WHY CULTS SUCCEED WHERE THE CHURCH FAILS

RONALD M. ENROTH
AND
J. GORDON MELTON

BRETHREN PRESS
Elgin, Illinois

Why Cults Succeed Where the Church Fails

Brethren Press, 1451 Dundee Avenue, Elgin, IL 60120

Cover design by Kathy Kline

Edited by Leslie R. Keylock

Library of Congress Cataloging in Publication Data

Enroth, Ronald M., and Melton, J. Gordon
    Why cults succeed where the church fails.

    Bibliography: p.
    1. Cults. 2. Religions. 3. Heresy. I. Melton, J. Gordon.
II. Title.
BL80.2.E56 1985   261.2   84-29272
ISBN 0-87178-931-0

Printed in the United States of America

WHY CULTS SUCCEED WHERE THE CHURCH FAILS

Contents

1

WHAT ARE CULTS?

Question: What are your basic differences with each other in your understanding of the cults?

ENROTH: As a jumping off place, let me make an observation, based on a quotation from one of Dr. Melton's books—*The Cult Experience:* "If one has a religious stance that assumes a person of another faith is either deluded by false teachers or inspired by demonic forces, then a negative interpretation of a person's involvement in a religious group that is outside the national religious consensus is guaranteed."

I come from the perspective of viewing the cults and their impact on individuals and families as basically negative and deleterious. I think that's the case primarily because it's my view that the cults' basic assumptions, their truth claims, are anchored in theological error. I'm very concerned about the distinction between truth and error with regard to the teachings and doctrines of cultic groups. I do not see that same concern in Dr. Melton's work. I think that's a major difference.

I have been identified with the "anticult" camp. "Anticult" is a term I have some problems with, but quite clearly my stance has been that cultic groups are essentially, though not entirely, destructive in nature. I feel strongly that cult leaders are, to use biblical terminology, false teachers and false prophets, and that some of their activity and some of their statements reveal real demonic forces. I think that that framework explains much of what I define as their negative impact.

I think our approaches to cults with regard to field research and the kinds of methodologies that are employed in the research process also probably differ. I am a sociologist and I'm therefore very concerned about objectivity and the need to get as much data as possible on the groups under discussion. However, I also feel very strongly about the importance of integrating one's faith and one's discipline. That's one reason I'm teaching at a Christian college. I must necessarily wear two hats—the hat of an objective scholar/sociologist, and the hat of a concerned evangelical Christian.

From my persective, looking at some of Dr. Melton's work, I see very little of the evangelical Christian/biblical critique in his work. I see some very good scholarship and an important approach to religious movements that's based on some very fine research. I can resonate with that. But I think that the value judgments that characterize my writing are largely absent in his, and that probably represents a third basic difference of approach. I feel that Christians need (in addition to approaching new religions or cults academically) to bring a clearly Christian or biblical critique to bear on these groups. Christian cult watchers, as they evaluate Gordon's work, see very, very little in the way of a specific biblical critique of the groups commonly known as cults.

MELTON: I think Dr. Enroth has, in part, hit the nail on the head, and I would agree that he has pinpointed where our basic differences begin. I believe this difference stems from our differing histories and approaches. I have been very uncomfortable with the whole term "cult" and only used it with great reluctance, even in my last book. I don't break groups down sociologically into cults, sects, denominations—I've found that to be an unworkable way of viewing groups. Rejecting that approach has had a major effect upon my research, because instead of saying, "Here is a group we'll call a 'cult,'" I've found myself saying, "Here is a group from the New Thought religions," and "Here is a group from the occult religions."

Other groups would be classified as Buddhist or Hindu.

So at the beginning I tend to see groups much more in their particularity. I think we make a great mistake in lumping them together because in so doing we assume that they have the same or similar characteristics that they don't share. Different groups that we have called cults are vastly different from each other. They differ in organization and have different recruitment techniques and belief structures. In short, they differ at every level.

Ron is also quite right that I have done, at least in print, very little Christian critique of such groups. There are several reasons for this. First, having grown up with the more traditional anticult literature (Irvine, Van Baalen, Haldeman), I used it as I began my own research. In the process I found a basic shallowness and frequent errors, especially in reporting the beliefs of groups. In effect, their critique was a strawman critique. They were critiquing something that did not exist, critiquing beliefs the group did not hold. Thus I came to feel it very important to find out what any particular group really believed, what it is really doing, what the logic of its inner workings is, why it seems so strange to us that people do the things they do. Why do Hare Krishnas shave their heads and go dancing in the street? Discovering such inner logic can rarely be done merely by reading one or two books that a group has published.

Thus before I critique a group I need to find out what it really believes, what its side of the story on a point of controversy is, how it would answer its critics. Frequently, for example, I will send what I have written about a group to the group itself and ask them if I have misrepresented them. Such checking is of great importance to me.

Second, I have refrained from a lot of Christian critiquing because so many groups are clearly outside the Christian framework, and doing a Christian theological critique of them seems superfluous. It's obvious that Hindus aren't Christians, and obvious that they do not hold evangelical Christian doctrines at any level. Reiterating that point continually does not seem to me to be of great value.

Measuring alternative religions is relatively simple when you are dealing with Christian deviations because they have deviated from a common base. When you are concerned with non-Christian groups, there is no common base or belief or no common authority to which each appeal. Buddhists don't just deviate from Christianity, they differ. They don't disbelieve a few essential doctrines or hold a few heretical notions, they don't believe anything we do. A search for a common ground from which we can begin to talk is very difficult. The average Buddhist is an atheist. Such a person does not believe in a God of any kind.

And I have, not being a theologian—and I make no claim to be one—a difficult task in sorting through doctrinal questions to do an adequate theological analysis of most groups' beliefs. I'm a church historian with most of my theological work in historical theology, not systematics. That's part of where I'm coming from.

I also have another problem, and it is related to where we are going later on. I have a problem as to where to draw the line —what's heresy and what's evangelically kosher. What is acceptable doctrinal deviation? Evangelicals have no common line. For example, I rely a great deal on the Religious Analysis Bureau. But it assumes that Pentecostalism is a heresy. Right along with its books on Moonies and Mormons, its catalog lists numerous titles attacking Pentecostalism. In my Christian world, while I am not one, I include Pentecostals in. I have no problems with my fellow believers in the Assemblies of God, the Church of God (Cleveland, Tennessee), or the Pentecostal Holiness Church. Yet, I have one book by a Pentecostal Holiness leader calling the theology of the Assemblies of God "the devil's counterfeit offer." I'm not a Pentecostal. I don't believe the way they do on basic issues. But I am not going to point my finger at them and say, "You're a heretic, and your opinion about the baptism of the Holy Spirit is going to keep us from fellowship."

There are numerous places where the issue of fellowship gets to be crucial. I have problems when I encounter the Eastern Orthodox, or especially a group like the Armenian Church, long condemned as Monophysite heretics but who themselves claim to be merely pre-Nicean. I have trouble drawing the line, and I tend to be inclusivistic instead of exclusivistic. I tend to say to individuals in "heretical" groups, "You are my Christian brothers and sisters. You are my erring Christian brothers and sisters, and we must talk about your error, but nonetheless you are brothers and sisters."

Finally, I also recognize my own differences. I'm a Methodist. I don't believe in predestination, at least in the sense that my Calvinist friends do. My forefathers in Methodism got all worked up about predestination. They said it led to antinomianism. Even as a Methodist church historian, however, I just can't get worked up about the topic. I just don't believe in it.

The situation changes the closer you get to home. For example, when you are dealing with a group such as The Way International, which presents itself as a biblically-based evangelical organization, it is important to know that The Way departs from orthodox Christian faith at several important points. More importantly, when one has a group that uses Christian language and symbols but that has placed these symbols into what is clearly a completely different religious structure (and I would include the Liberal Catholic Church and the Unification Church in this category), it behooves us to point out the true nature of that group's theological base.

Thus we can see the basic difference between the way Ron and I approach the problem. To me the term "cult" is obsolete and is at best a handy little catchword that describes a simple sociological reality, namely, there are some religions that deviate from the norm of a given culture so much that they are playing a different religious ball game. If you go to India, Methodists and Presbyterians and Baptists are cults and are so treated because they are completely outside the mainstream of Indian religion. The established religious leaders see them as being led by a bunch of false teachers, and in places have led in curtailing their activities by legal means. So that's one difference.

However, I might add, I have developed a belief, a kind of working hypothesis, that if you lay out what people really believe, just simply lay it out, frequently the absurdities of it come to the fore, and there is no need to belabor those absurdities. For example, I find myself in particular disagreement with the Southern Methodist Church, possibly because I am a United Methodist who lived through the troubles of the church in the south in the 1960s. In any case, this group has a clearly stated policy of racial apartheid. Yet, when I wrote about the Southern Methodists, I merely stated that segregation was a policy of theirs. I did not think there was any point in saying I didn't like that. Obviously I don't. I think people are intelligent enough to react properly if they have the correct information.

I have also followed this kind of format in presenting the more controversial of the "cults." I try to delineate the more significant of the charges brought against any group, as well as any answer to those charges. If a controversy has been resolved clearly, I also try to present that information. Recently, I did an article for *Christianity Today*, in which I discussed the nature of the Moonie wedding and the results to the church of the July 1982 ceremony at Madison Square Garden. Here, without wasting ink on unnecessary diatribes against Moon, I presented his family history (which I do not see as a model for family life) and, without condemning those Unificationists who follow Moon's thinking about marriage, I demonstrated why it was not an acceptable Christian alternative. Along the way, I also tried to demonstrate how the marriage system differed from its public image of merely a situation in which Moon arbitrarily and capriciously tells each member who to marry.

ENROTH: I don't think there's really a major difference between us with regard to the problems that often come with using the word "cult." I don't see a difference between us concerning the importance of distinguishing between the various groups that have been called cults. I am the first to admit that the word "cult" is a very ambiguous, "sticky" term that means many things to many people. In fact, I make a statement in the book *A Guide to Cults and New Religions* that the word "cult" has become a blurred designation. It's a very blurred term; yet it's a popular term. It's in our everyday usage. I agree with Jim Sire who asked whether or not its usefulness has been diminished to the point where perhaps we should stop using it. He states: "We should if we could, but we can't—I think we're stuck with it." The man on the street, the person in the pew, identifies with the word "cult." I teach a course called "New Religious Movements"—but my students refer to it as the "cult course." I certainly recognize that "cult" is a less-than-precise term. I also see the need for distinguishing between the various kinds of new religions. I've made distinctions between the Eastern/mystical groups, the aberrational Christian groups, the self-improvement or transformational cults, the psychic/occult/astral cults, and the eclectic cults—the groups that combine elements of various religions into a new form.

So, in short, I'm very much aware of the need to distinguish between cults. I think one of the problems some people have with regard to cults is to see them as a unitary phenomenon, not having differences. Although cults vary a great deal one from another, they also have some patterns of behavior and certain characteristics that apply to most if not all, of them. As a sociologist, I'm interested in recurring patterns of behavior with regard to leadership, with regard to the recruitment and socialization of members, as well as with many other areas of cult life. I see the differences, but I also see the similarities.

MELTON: What would be the patterns that would run through the cults—the Krishnas, the Moonies, Wicca, the Church of Religious Science?

ENROTH: The kinds of patterns I see there would be, first of all, a strong authoritarian presence, an emphasis on the leader-founder, a focal emphasis on the leader's teachings, and the elevation of the leaders to a very high position of respect, sometimes bordering on deity. From the Christian perspective, there is obviously a departure from revealed truth as we understand it, and in that sense a pattern of false teaching. I see from my perspective as a sociologist an oppositional or adversarial stance vis-à-vis the major social institutions of our society. Another common trait would be the element of control over the lives of members. Control mechanisms operate not only in the Eastern or more exotic cultic groups, but also in those sects much closer to home. Even in groups that call themselves Christian you can see these same characteristics of control and manipulation. You can't always distinguish between "Eastern" and "Christian" with regard to some of the sociological phenomena. I see a theme of elitism, an exclusivistic orientation with regard to not only their teachings but also their conveying a sense of superiority that is linked perhaps to their view of their own group as being central to history.

Those are the kinds of central features that I would see as characterizing all these groups.

MELTON: I would find myself agreeing with at least some of what you have said—the adversarial role vis-à-vis social institutions, almost a definition of what we're talking about, as well as the criteria of false (vis-à-vis evangelical Christianity) teachings.

I tend to see strong authority to be not so much a characteristic of "cults" but of any first-generation religion. It's a characteristic shared by "Pope" John Wesley, the heavy-handed Francis Asbury, Cotton Mather and the ministers of seventeenth-century New England, and of Brigham Young, who welded the Utah Mormons into a tightly-knit organization.

During the second generation, after the founder-leader is gone, the groups will move into a strong bureaucracy (the way Christian Science has gone) or slide into a looser organization such as Alexander Dowie's Christian Catholic Church. You can see the shift in the Hare Krishnas, who moved with a twenty-person governing authority that replaced the single leadership of Swami Bhaktivedanta in the mid-1970s.

I see first-generation religion as essentially having a strong leader. It is very characteristic of a person or a small group of people to initiate a new religious organization and to keep control of it during his or her lifetimes.

ENROTH: But isn't there a difference between Moon and John Wesley? Moon's authority rests in his office, his role as the

Lord of the Second Advent or Messiah, the key figure in the Second Coming of Christ—whereas John Wesley certainly didn't make those kinds of claims for himself. Although they're both in a sense authoritarian leaders, and certainly strong leaders, I think one must make a distinction between someone like Moon and a Wesley because of the very significant differences in who they claim to be and how their followers relate to them.

MELTON: Certainly Moon and Wesley are different, especially if we talk in terms of false teaching. But in terms of authority, or of how they were seen by their contemporaries, we see some similarities. Wesley was viewed as a "cultist." He was actually called an "enthusiast." Wesley assumed the title of bishop, about which the Church of England became very upset. He then proceeded to write a book about why he was a bishop, and he claimed to be one simply on the basis of his work and accomplishments, not on the basis of formal apostolic succession. He deserved the title. When one considers the different conditions of their times and speaks narrowly of their strong assertion of authority (self-proclaimed) and their adversarial role vis-à-vis established social institutions, Wesley and Moon show some important parallels. They come off very close to each other.

I think strong leadership tends to be that way, i.e., first-generation leadership tends to be very strong, as people try to perpetuate their particular religious vision. And, of course, Wesley was considered by his cohorts as very much the theological radical and outcast, preaching all sorts of "heresy," ideas that some evangelicals still consider heresy.

Question: How do you view the issue of a cult group's elitism?

MELTON: Elitism is an issue affecting religious groups of all stripes. Within each community you can find groups that consider themselves an elite. Many Christian groups tend to be this way. Unificationists see themselves this way, as do the Krishnas.

There are other groups, including some "cults," that are

quite the opposite. They tend to be very inclusivistic. Most Hindu groups fit that pattern. They tend to say that everybody's really a part of us. They claim to be practicing "religion itself," whereas we Christians are merely a particular expression of a religion, we have yet to grasp the pure essence of religiousness. We are only partly Hindu.

If you shift slightly from the issue of elitism to the related issue of exclusivism, a similar pattern emerges. You can place orthodox groups, sect groups, or cult groups on a gigantic exclusiveness-inclusiveness scale. It's a characteristic of all religious groups—from Carl McIntire's Bible Presbyterian Church to the United Methodist Church—to fit on a spectrum from the separatist "we-are-it" churches to the kinds that seem to say, "Everybody can come, no standards necessary." You have the same spectrum in the cults. On the one end are those who you only know about because ten people who are the rulers of the world in secret do something that gets them into the newspaper; otherwise they're off by themselves, alone. Other groups are visibly open to whoever will join them and are happy to have anyone.

The point is that cults do not have a corner on the exclusivist-elitist market. Every major group I know has got a little bit of cosmic history in its world. Evangelical Christians really think they're the center of creation. I think I am at the center— I'm part of what is really happening in the universe because I am a Christian and I know that God has chosen the church of which I am a part to play a key role in history. I also know a lot of people who disagree with me, some of whom believe their group is at the center.

But while I do not think elitism or exclusivism particularly characterizes cults, there is one characteristic I do find generally a part of their life: first-century Christian zeal. That is, they think that, small as they are and as unsuccessful as they have been in their first years of existence, they're still going to rule the world. They are the religion of the future. It may not be in our lifetime, they tell me, it may be two or three generations, or even, as Moon's people have put it, five hundred years, but eventually we're going to make it. We are the wave of the future. That's something I find among the Wiccans. Now there's a little bitty group. You go and look at them, and the first thing you notice is that they worship these deities that seem to have died two thousand years ago. You wonder at the archaic nature of it all. Then you talk to them. They really believe that Pagan religion is coming back and is the wave of the future. They believe they will live to see it as once again a major religion of the world.

The Pagans struck a nerve as I listened to them, because I have seen so many discouraged Christians who have lost that sense of Christianity as the wave of the future. I'm almost looking forward to some of our African and Korean brothers and sisters coming over here and giving us that sense again—those seem to be two of the few places in the world that still have it.

Question: You agree that there are certain characteristics that could be used to describe cults . . .

MELTON: My basic approach to a new group, a cult, is neutral. I suspect that my background as a geologist prepared me for my work, but I try to approach a cult as a new social organism, much as a biologist would approach a new species. I ask myself, "What does this group do? What effects does it cause?" Only after first approaching it and trying to understand it do I proceed to any evaluation. But then I have two different sets of standards by which I evaluate the group.

One set of standards is fairly secular. As a secular organism, as a social organism, such as the corporation down the street or the local social club, as a purely secular entity, what are its effects? Is it basically a good group or a bad group? In other words, does it help people, hurt people, or generally just take up their time? Overwhelmingly, on this level, I find that the worst thing I can say about most groups is that for a few years they waste people's time.

Also, in probing the inner workings of some groups you find some have significant defects. I like to check the records of leaders. Do their records disclose problems that lead you to question their sincerity? Does the leader really believe what she or he is saying? Occasionally such questioning leads to real problems. For example, Paul Twitchell. The evidence that David Lane uncovered of Twitchell's creating a false history of his rise to leadership of ECKANKAR indicates extensive corruption. That the leadership has done nothing to correct Twitchell's false claims, yea, have perpetuated them, indicates a significant problem at the heart of that organization.

There are other groups I believe are doing harm to their members. I think there are some Eastern groups, for example, that are run by inept gurus (I also think there are some Baptist and Pentecostal congregations being run by inept pastors, by the way). Inept gurus do not understand their role in assisting people in life transformations. They tend to hold people in dependence and adolescence rather than assisting them to grow toward maturity and adulthood.

One's initial relation to a guru—in the West we would call that person a spiritual guide or counselor—is submission. The devotee submits to the guru to break the patterns of the past. But it should be a transitory submission that leads to a new freedom—much as the recruit submits to a basic training sergeant or a patient to a psychiatrist. The typical first encounter with a guru occurs around the movement from adolescence to adulthood. The encounter with a "good" authority figure (be it guru, pastor, college professor, army sergeant, or boss) assists many people to break out of the role of child. The encounter with a bad guru can stiffle that process for many years.

Overwhelmingly, however, I have discovered that the new religions are neither particularly good or bad. They are not doing anything, merely functioning as holding tanks for people while they work out problems on their own. It's of some interest to me that these groups came along right about the time we killed the draft, and that some of these groups are serving the same function that the army served, in terms of providing a bridge out of the childhood situation.

That discussion leads to family relations, another factor I

consider when observing groups. This area has been a major, if not *the* major issue inciting opposition to new religions. Middle class culture is having a rough time dealing with the transition of teen-agers to adulthood. We have the problem of families whose internal structure is so strong that teen-agers have a difficult time breaking free. In particular, they have a rough time cutting themselves off from the expectations of their parents that they cannot share or feel they cannot live up to. I tend to judge groups on how they handle their end of that very real and serious problem. I think, for example, that the Hare Krishnas have a history of handling that problem very poorly. Other groups, for example various yoga groups, have a much better record. Rajneesh handles this problem far better, in spite of his other problems.

Finally, violence is an issue with a few groups. Groups like Synanon and Ananda Marga have had a history of violent interaction with society. The Faith Assembly in Indiana has a history of family violence. In Ananda Marga's case, violence has taken the form of murders, mass murder in one case. Several years ago a mob in India broke into their meeting and killed seventeen members. Two members of Ananda Marga are now sitting in jail for having murdered a political official in Australia. A member in Sweden killed a guru who had left Ananda Marga and established a rival movement. Shot him dead. The guru had gone to Sweden thinking he was to address an assembly of potential followers. He stepped off the plane, and that was the last anyone ever saw of him alive. Several months later they found his body. While this violence has its origin in the political sitation in India, it has followed the movement around the world.

With the Faith Assembly—Hobart Freeman's group—the recently published stories of the high death rate in the group, their rejection of the use of doctors, babies who have died from simple neglect, indicate a real problem.

These are some of the criteria I use to judge groups by.

ENROTH: But you don't mention that in your writing. The destructive elements you're talking about right now, I think, are far more common than a person would gather from your own writing. You seem to neglect or gloss over what I consider to be the negative dimensions of cultic life.

MELTON: In *The Cult Experience* I don't, and I think you will see that in the last chapter. However, the problem is more complicated than it first appears. Reports of violence, what we have been calling destructive elements, have to be seen broadly in the larger context, and not simply used to denigrate a particular group or, more importantly, denigrate all groups because of the sins of one. For example, child abuse has recently been prominent in the news.

Child abuse is a national disgrace. It occurs in all segments of society and in most religious groups. The fact that it is generally absent from Eastern cult groups may be a significant fact. The fact that it seems to be more present in conservative evangelical Christian groups may or may not be significant data. It may just be that that's the data that got reported and picked up by the media. We must expect among Christian groups, being just one segment of the population, that there's going to be a certain amount of child beating, simply because child beaters are pretty liberally spread throughout our culture. There may not be a distinct relationship between child abuse and Christianity, except in the fact that any group that emphasizes the discipline of children and condones corporeal punishment would draw child beaters into it. Childbeaters would see the group's condoning of corporeal punishment as a sanction for their abusive behavior.

Child beating is passed on through the family; it's not passed on through religious groups. If you have people join your group (church or cult or whatever), they're going to beat their children whether they're in the group or out of the group or attached to no group or attached to any group.

But if they are members of an unpopular group, a cult, and if they beat their children and are discovered, and if someone reports their action, the media covers the incident. If a United Methodist beats a child, it's not reported that a Methodist child-beater is on the loose. If it is covered at all, the article will merely state that another person in the community is beating his or her children. Roman Catholics beat their children, but it's not reported that a Roman Catholic couple beat their children. There are more Roman Catholic childbeaters in this country than any other kind, simply because there are more Roman Catholics in the country than any other kind.

Data about destructive behavior has to be seen in conjunction with other relevant data.

ENROTH: What about the aberrational Christian groups that practice this regularly and who, because of their philosophy or world view, actually encourage this kind of behavior—and not just because the people happen to be Protestants.

MELTON: I think that society should come down heavily upon them for it, because they are violating the law.

ENROTH: For example, I know of a group called the "Body of Christ." It's very small and has never been mentioned in the newspapers or in books. I've read the literature they put out, and they come right out and say that children come between you and God. They may not physically abuse children, but they appear to neglect their children and relegate them to a lower status. They say that when you join their group, which they consider to be "God's family," all "natural affection" must go. God becomes your spouse. Your "natural" family ties must be severed, and the group becomes your family. Their own writings state that the term "natural affection" includes not only affection for wife, husband, and children, but also affection for pets. It's the only cult I've discovered in which the severing of relationships extends to animals.

Another example of this kind of thing can be found in the teaching of Ed Mitchell, head of the River of Life Ministry. He explicitly separates parents from children—segregates them. Mothers are told not to exhibit a "spirit of motherhood"—undue affection—toward their children. A former member of this group reports that she and her husband were placed in separate dormitories from their kids. Her young son fell one day and cut himself very badly, and she knew that he needed medical attention. The leaders would not allow her to show any caring attitude toward him. She wasn't even permitted to touch him or go near him. She was taught to suppress her natural inclination to care for and help him. Such behavior was redefined and spiritualized by the cult leader. In this group, womanhood and motherhood are dramatically (and I would say demonically) redefined as being a negative influence on people. Women are viewed as temptresses, and mothers who exhibit undue affection for their children come to see those children as "idols." In their twisted theology this groups says that such feelings are a barrier to true spirituality. Those kinds of things can be documented and are more commonplace than might be believed.

MELTON: Those kinds of things need to be dealt with forthrightly, and I have no problem with that. In fact, I heartily welcome it. We just have to see that any incident is characteristic of only one group, and we should not use it to hit other groups we define as cults.

ENROTH: But those kinds of behaviors are not reported by people like Jeff Hadden and Bromley and Shupe. Social scientists like them abhor the adjective "destructive" and despise the noun "cult." They distrust the accounts of former members and dismiss with seeming contempt what they term the "horror stories" of former cult members. I have real problems with that kind of "value free" sociology.

MELTON: You are quite correct. My feeling about that particular kind of thing is that it should be reported. One of the real problems we have on the national level is documenting such material. For example, you know about the "Body of Christ." You say it is a small group, not in the papers. You should take responsibility for reporting the information and reporting it in such a way that I sitting in Chicago can read it as something more than just another "horror" story of doubtful validity. The lack of such a flow of information—and I am as guilty as any of not reporting—is a major obstacle today.

ENROTH: The media do not pick up on a small group of less than a hundred members. They're not interested unless it's a particularly unique or exotic story.

MELTON: We need a system of monographs, a place to write up four or five pages and get it out to people, and we can know the information can be trusted. There are some sources whose information I simply cannot use unless and until it is verified by another independent source. For example, I would never use a news account or story from the *Advisor*, recently re-titled *The Cult Observer* (the periodical of the American Family Foundation), or any information disseminated by the Citizens Freedom Foundation (another secular anticult group). Both have published too many items that have turned out to be false rumors or just plain incorrect accounts of incidents.

And of course there is the additional problem of getting that one verifiable account that can be used. The work hours it takes to do that are unbelievable. I imagine you can look back on your relationship with that one group and the many (how many?) hours it took you to gather the information. Multiply that by the number of other reported incidents, and it becomes a real problem of investigation and getting the information out.

ENROTH: But those instances can be cited, too, for the larger, better known groups. Let me mention one example from the Unification Church and their alleged use of "heavenly deception" with regard to fund raising and recruiting. You correctly point out, Gordon, that the northern California branch of the Moonies (the Oakland Family) is especially guilty of using deceptive tactics. But the point is that there are other instances of "heavenly deception" Moonies have used in other parts of the country.

Here is an example that a former student of mine personally witnessed in Denver. He was walking along a street in that city when he was approached by a young woman who was soliciting funds, she said, for a Christian organization called "Youth Guidance." She said that the organization worked with predelinquent young people, teen-agers who had had a few scrapes with the law. She did not identify herself in any way with the Unification Church.

As you may know, Youth Guidance is in fact a subdivision

of Youth for Christ. After the young woman had made her appeal, my friend took out his card identifying himself as the director of Youth Guidance in the city of Denver and indicated that he did not recognize the young woman as being a staff member of his organization. He asked to see her ID, and she turned all kinds of shades of red. He pressed her, and she finally admitted that she was a member of the Unification Church. She seemed to be engaging in fraudulent misrepresentation—a very serious matter. From her perspective, however, it was merely a case of "heavenly deception" wherein the end justifies the means.

When I mentioned this incident sometime later to the president of the Unification Church in the United States, he said, in essence, "Oh, well, that's a very isolated incident. It perhaps happened; I'm not denying the possibility. It shouldn't have happened, and we don't condone that kind of thing. It was probably an overzealous Asian or someone who comes out of an Eastern cultural tradition and who has tremendous loyalty feelings toward the leader."

In my opinion, his response was pure rationalization, an attempt at what sociologists call the neutralization of deviance.

While I'm not saying that all Moonies engage in this kind of thing all the time, I maintain that there are more than a few isolated instances of deceitful practices that have been reported, and they are not restricted to the San Francisco Bay Area Moonies.

Let me cite one more illustration from Santa Barbara, California—my own city. When the Moonies had their headquarters in a little Victorian house on Chapala Street, they placed a sign in the window that said, simply, "Help Wanted." There was no other sign or indication that the building was a Unification Center. That "Help Wanted" sign seems to have been deceptive, because I'm quite sure its main function was to serve as a hook to get people to come inside. A lot of young people are walking the streets looking for work, and it's quite possible that that recruitment ploy met with some success.

Cultic groups have been known to place ads in the classified sections of newspapers—ads that do not reveal the true identity of the group. They offer positions involving "community work" or describe vague jobs "helping people" and state that living expenses, including medical expenses, are paid by the group. "Interviews start Monday. Call . . . ."

My point is that this kind of deceptive practice actually takes place. Yet writers like Bromley and Shupe in *Strange Gods*, as well as you in your writings, rarely mention this dimension of the cult experience. These particular social scientists say that allegations of deceptive practices have been exaggerated. I disagree. I think we have to call a spade a spade and not fall for the public relations pitch of those cults that seek to minimize and downplay such behavior when confronted with evidence of deceit.

2

WHAT ABOUT DEPROGRAMMING?

Question: How do you feel about deprogramming, "exit counseling," and other similar "anticult" practices?

MELTON: Let me begin my answer with some preliminary observations. Within the whole area of cults and anticultism we as Christians must be in a position of continually giving an account of our faith, continually letting people know where we're coming from, why we're coming from there, and why certain beliefs and practices are no-nos. In relation to the cults, in particular, we have quite an education program to do, a difficult problem at best, and mainline churches aren't interested in this area at all. But it's an important task we have to accomplish.

I see the task as one primarily of distinguishing our teachings, our faith, from heterodox Christianity. More work needs to be done, especially in areas where the differences appear to be subtle but are nevertheless very important. For example, we need to explain to our people why we are Trinitarian and not Arian. And the most challenging force that I have encountered is Gnosticism. I think Gnosticism is the main contemporary challenge to the faith with which we have to deal, especially inside the church. In relation to Gnosticism, as one example, we have both a polemical and an apologetic role. We must deal with the claims of yoga to be a science, the claims of TM or the exponents of reincarnation to scientific verification. In other words, we must call attention to the claims of various groups that their teachings are undergirded with science, especially when that science is at best very weak. (By the way, it is this task that I feel justifies above all else my writing for *Fate* Magazine. While I am not able to "preach," I have been able to spend much of my space pointing out the weaknesses in the claims of TM, reincarnationism, Carlos Castaneda's teaching, Edgar Cayce's writings, etc. Writing for a large readership that will never look at a book published by a Christian publishing house, I feel I have a unique opportunity and ministry.)

ENROTH: Just a comment on something you said—"We need to let people know where we're coming from as Christians." I agree. Part of the problem those of us in the so-called Christian cult-watching circles have with you is that we don't know where you're coming from. At least in writing you have not made it very clear as to precisely where you're coming from. You now say that we need to be concerned about the claims of TM, whether or not it's scientific, and we need to be concerned about some of these other things as Christians. I don't think you've put that in writing.

I think that earlier you said, regarding Eastern religions, that it's not important to distinguish them from Christianity, that that was not one of your emphases. Most of the rest of us Christian cult watchers would see it as important to look at and identify the basic assumptions, for example, of an Eastern mystical occult world view and distinguish that world view from an orthodox, biblical Christian view. We feel that it is necessary to help people in and outside the church to see the intrusion of this occult-mystical world view into our culture under the guise of self-improvement groups like est, Lifespring, Scientology, and Transcendental Meditation.

Question: Dr. Melton, why do you see Gnosticism as the major challenge to Christianity today?

MELTON: I see a significant growth in a theology that denies the Incarnation. It denies the Word made flesh at all levels. It denies the importance of Jesus and his ministry and work of salvation, and substitutes a vague thing called the "Christ principle," which really becomes anything you want it to be. In the end it is very selfish and egocentric in its approach to human beings. It goes so much for individual religious experience that it costs us Christian community.

Question: Could you give some specifics?

MELTON: I'm thinking of New Thought metaphysics, and the New Age Movement. I am also thinking of the sweetness and light approach of much conservative Christianity whose Gnosticism shows up as, to quote a popular gospel song, "Me and Jesus got our own thing going, we don't need anybody to tell us what it's all about," and the world is forgotten. Such an attitude is Gnosticism pure and simple. There's where I see the main challenge and main ministry of anticult activity.

I might also add that we need a much more perceptive analysis of the New Age Movements one free of the distraction of unprovable conspiracy theories such as that offered in Constance Cumbey's *Hidden Dangers of the Rainbow*, which gives little help in either the diagnosis or the treatment of Gnosticism-run-rampant.

But getting back to the main thrust of the question, when anticult activity goes beyond its apologetic and polemical roles, and when Christians move from their basic task of witnessing to the gospel, I see danger. Especially when such activity moves into attempts to pass legislation against particular religious groups (i.e., cults), or moves into coercive action against cult members, or meddles in the internal affairs of different groups, I begin to have real problems.

As to deprogramming, I think my feelings are pretty well known. I think of deprogrammers in the same way as I think of rapists, and I think the same thing should be done to each of them—they should be tossed into jail for the public protection.

I make no bones about that opinion. I no longer even think of deprogrammers as people with whom I have an honest difference of opinion. I think of them—and by them I refer not to the parents who for all kinds of mixed reasons turn to them but to those who actively deprogram and support deprogrammers—as criminals engaged in illegal and antisocial activity.

Deprogramming is nothing less than a violation of everything we stand for in this country in terms of individual freedom and rights. I think the whole business about mind control and brainwashing is hogwash, intellectual hogwash. I see no evidence that members of cults or authoritarian Christian churches or other authoritarian groups have lost any ability to think or that they have not chosen to be a part of the group. I see no evidence that they have been illegitimately "lured" into the group instead of choosing to be a part of it.

Having had my say about deprogramming, I would want to emphasize that I feel just as strongly in favor of any kind of noncoercive counseling that would assist people who are trying to decide about leaving or, even more so, counseling in situations where a family conflict exists. A family may want a family member to leave a religious group. There are well-known family counseling procedures for such conflicts.

I am also in favor—I do it a lot myself—of direct witnessing to non-Christians and non-Christian groups about the claims of the gospel. My main problem with some of my Christian brothers and sisters at this point is the flavor of open hostility that they often exude toward such groups, and by extension toward group members, in their witnessing. I do not believe that approaching a cult member with insults about the group or leader, insults that question the integrity of anyone who would join such a group, is either helpful or particularly Christian. In witnessing to cult members we must above all things broadcast the love of Jesus, which should be the keynote of our lives. Cult members are people we hope to win to Christ. They are not the principalities and powers of darkness that we rightfully rebuke. I say to each Christian concerned with heresy: *the greatest heresy, greater than Gnosticism, Arianism or Pelagianism, is lack of love.*

That reflection raises the question of the differences between Christian and secular anticultists. I sometimes make that distinction, but I more frequently use the term "militant anticultism." By millitant I refer to people and groups—Christian, secular, or otherwise—who support deprogramming and legislation specifically aimed at destroying cults. The resulting distinction between militant and nonmilitant anticultists cuts across the Christian-secular line. The borders are vague. For example, Spiritual Counterfeits Project has in several of its publications said that it does not support deprogramming. At the same time its newsletter gave a favorable review to the book *Snapping*. I remember writing Brooks Alexander on that particular issue, asking him how SCP could support such an anti-Christian book as *Snapping* and give it such a favorable review. And although Brooks comes out against "deprogramming," he supports taking a person forcefully out of a group for something called "reality testing." That sounds very much like deprogramming to me.

While I would like to think that militant anitcultism was confined to secular anticult groups, or at least that evangelical anticult groups were free of militancy, I see too much evidence to the contrary. Joel MacCollam, who had a chapter in Ron's last book, is an active deprogrammer. Baptist minister George Swope heads, or at least did head (he has been ordered by the court to cease and desist), a deprogramming group and "rehabilitation" (and I use that term loosely) center in New England. Joseph Hopkins, who wrote the only negative review I received of *The Cult Experience*, chose to publish it in *The Advisor*. In a recent issue of *The Discerner*, lo, after these many years, even the Religious Research Bureau, who I have found a vital source of information for many years, came out in an editorial in support of deprogramming. I couple this support of militant anticultism by people I identify as evangelical voices with the fact that, until recently, others have remained silent on the issue. I, of course, welcome the recent statements of yourself, Walter Martin and James Bjornstad. At the same time, in the 1970s, it was terribly lonesome. I could have used that support when deprogramming was at its height and legislation was actually pending.

So I see a distinction between secular and anticult activity and the work of Christian witnessing and countercult endeavors. However, on a day-to-day basis the important distinction has been between militant and nonmilitant. I have unfortunately found too many Christians, even evangelical Christian leaders, who have identified with the militant anticult movement to be able to say that the militants are confined to the secular anticultists. So when I speak of militant anticultists, I mean those people, known and unknown, who support coercive deconversion and legislation against a select list of unpopular religious groups.

I see legislative attempts as really dangerous today. Today's enemies can very easily become tomorrow's friends. Legislation we pass today against cults could be both used against us tomorrow or more likely become a precedent for passing future anti-religious legislation that would be turned upon us.

The other side of the coin of publishing material on the negative aspects of a cult or cult life should also be highlighted. Tracking down and disconfirming false rumors is a serious problem and has become a major time-consuming task because of the anticult movement. Here I refer to the secular anticult movement as opposed to the Christian countercult movement.

Question: Maybe, Dr. Melton, this would be the place to expand on the distinction you're making, since many readers are not going to be familiar with the distinctions between the secular anticultists and Christian countercult efforts.

MELTON: The Christian countercult movement began in the critique of nonevangelical Christianity in the early part of this century by fundamentalists (most notably Plymouth Brethren) and was carried on primarily by Reformed and Baptist writers. By the end of World War II evangelical opinions on the major dissenting groups such as Jehovah's Witnesses and the Mormons had become quite established. Since World War II a number of institutes and ministries engaged in research and witnessing efforts to members of nonevangelical groups have been founded. These organizations are managed and staffed by evangelical Christians, and they offer an evangelical appraisal of non-Christian religions and heretical Christian churches.

I think immediately, to mention a few examples, of the Spiritual Counterfeits Project, which is by far the best of approximately one hundred such separate organizations. I have had the longest running knowledge of and attachment to the Religious Bureau of Research in Minneapolis. The books it provides and its magazine, *The Discerner*, have been a major source of information for my research. It has been around for over twenty-five years. More recently-formed groups would include CARIS (Christian Apologetics: Research and Information Service), the Institute of Contemporary Christianity, and PACE (Practical Apologetics and Christian Evangelism).

The secular groups are very new. They grew up in the 1970s out of the work of Ted Patrick and the Citizens Freedom Foundation. CFF remains the largest of the secular groups, though it has recently been joined by the American Family Foundation, whose magazine *The Cult Observer* (formerly *The Advisor*) is probably the major anticult periodical today.

Unlike the Christian countercult groups, which tend to be very broad in their concern, the secular groups have developed a very narrow focus. Christian groups, except those few that were formed by a small group of former members of a single cult (i.e., Ex-Mormons for Jesus), have tended to offer a broad ministry to non-Christians and have tried to speak to many different groups. The secular anticultists, while talking about the mythical five thousand cults, put all their energy into a relative few, about fifteen or twenty.

Question: Why have they chosen to center in on this narrow group?

MELTON: Basically because these twenty groups have been most successful in recruiting white middle-class to upper-middle-class young adults. Parents have been very upset because in the recruitment process the new members left school, short-circuited a career, cut off engagements, and broke off relationships with their family. The concerns of parents have been the heart of, have fueled and financed, the secular anticult movement. I might add, both because I am a parent and because I have counseled with many parents whose sons and daughters have joined an alternative religion, that I have a real sympathy with the concerns that have motivated the anticult movement. I do, however, strongly disapprove of its methods and tactics in trying to destroy the groups it sees as enemies, specifically deprogramming and seeking legislation against religious groups it defines as cults.

But to return to the matter of false rumors, the literature produced by secular anticultists is filled with page after page of negative reports on various cults. Unfortunately, a high percentage of that material is merely the reprinting of false rumors, half-truths, and unverified statements. I have spent much of my time as a researcher tracking down such reports. Once it gets in print, especially if it is mentioned in a major information source such as the *New York Times*, it becomes very hard to correct. We used to hear a lot of rumors, for example, of paramilitary training in The Way International and of the stockpiling of weapons by the Krishnas, but when we tracked down the full story, it came out much differently.

As the stories appeared concerning the Krishnas, first of all, we heard of leaders who had been caught with a bunch of weapons and of a sheriff who had gone on a gun search at one of the temples. We heard of guns at a farm in West Virginia. That story seemed to be a contradiction, since the Krishnas are pacifists. We waited, and there was no follow-up to the initial stories. Eventually the San Francisco papers did carry a follow-up story, but it was not picked up across the country. Several researchers particularly interested in the Krishnas had looked into the case, and here's what they discovered. One of the leaders, before he joined the Hare Krishna movement, had been a gun collector. The movement had told him to get rid of his weapons. He refused. He was disciplined. He was then caught with the guns in the trunk of his car. He was further disciplined, stripped of his power, and eventually kicked out of the movement.

In this case a member of the group was being disciplined by the group for going against the group's policy at the time he got caught. It was not the Kirshnas in this case, it was one member who was a dissident within the movement, though he had risen to a position of some authority.

A similar set of interrelated incidents that began with some outsiders firing shotguns into the temple in West Virginia and threatening to kill the community leader stood behind the reports from West Virginia. The massive stockpile of weapons consisted of but two .22 rifles that had never been fired.

The Way International has also suffered under many repeated accusations that it was training members in guerilla warfare. That rumor was repeated by several reporters who should have known better. In fact, The Way had been teaching a program at its college in gun safety, a program designed for hunters established and funded by the state of Kansas. Here was a case of a half-truth that was distorted into a falsehood, pure and simple. (The same problem permeates every aspect of the history of the Church of Scientology.)

We thus have both tasks. We have the task of reporting accurately the negative facts that are facts. Many of the major alternative religions have facts in their history that I am sure they would rather forget. For example, I am very aware of the Krishna's responsibility in the disappearance of David Yanoff. The Church of Scientology must bear responsibility for the actions of the Guardians office (and, incidently, in his last annual report Hubbard admitted such responsibility).

But we also have the job of tracking down and reporting on all the unverified reports and false rumors that have been presented as facts. That's a real problem.

Take the issue of deceptive recruiting Ron mentioned earlier. That's often one characteristic we assign to cults. But when we tracked down the stories of deceptive recruiting, they all went to one place: the Oakland Family of the Unification Church. Anybody who knows anything about the Unification Church knows that the Oakland Family was atypical of Moonie groups. If Moshe Durst had not been promoted to president of the church, the Oakland Family would have probably splintered from the main movement. It was certainly different. Their tactics varied considerably from the rest of the church.

ENROTH: I recognize the distinction Gordon was mentioning between the Christian and the secular anticult movement, but he doesn't, unfortunately, make the distinction in his published writing. We're all painted with the same brush. The term that he and others use regularly is "militant anticultism." There's no distinction made between the Christian research organization—Spiritual Counterfeits Project, for example—and the Citizens Freedom Foundation, the nonsectarian parents' organization Gordon mentioned earlier.

A case in point is the book *Strange Gods: The Great American Cult Scare* by David G. Bromley and Anson D. Shupe, Jr. On the first page of that book the authors mention an "anticult" coalition, including the "fundamentalist" Spiritual Counterfeits Project, whose members are all "united in their opposition to cults." Lowell D. Streiker in his book *Mind-Bending: Brainwashing, Cults and Deprogramming in the Eighties* engages in a similar "lumping" process in his discussion of the anticult network.

Now I know that Gordon sees the distinctions between the Christian and the secular groups, but the point is he doesn't make that distinction in writing. He uses the general terms "anticult" or "militant anticult movement." I think he needs to distinguish more clearly between what are sometimes very important differences within the so-called anticult movement.

I also agree with Gordon that there have been some rumors about cultic groups that have been falsely circulated and cannot be substantiated. This is a very emotion-laden topic, and there's a lot of misinformation floating around. I'm the first to admit that. At the same time I think that Gordon's camp does not sufficiently stress the facts that *have* been verified with regard to the truly negative aspects of cults.

The critics of the anticult movement need to give serious attention to the widespread allegations of psychological and physical abuse in the cults. Independent verification of some of these allegations has already been made, especially with regard to the medical neglect of children in groups like Hobart Freeman's Faith Assembly. Faith Tabernacle, headed by Eleanor Daries, has reportedly inflicted various forms of abuse on members—adults as well as children. It is a small and unknown group that has received no media attention.

On the other hand, the East-Coast-based Church of Bible Understanding made the newspapers with regard to violence. A young teen-ager was so badly beaten by the elders that he was admitted to a hospital in Philadelphia. This is on record. It's been verified by medical authorities. It is not unverified rumor but verified fact.

My contention is that the opponents of the so-called anticult movement have not really been honest with the facts and have emphasized so much the rumors that have not been verified, with regard to Moon and his alleged sexual activities, for example, that they have neglected a broad spectrum of verifiable data about both well-known and less well-known groups.

There are many groups, some of them very small (such as the River of Life Ministry), that regularly engage in destructive behavior vis-à-vis families and individuals. Much of the information about such behavior comes from former members.

This brings up an important difference between Gordon and myself. I have been criticized, along with others who have written critically about the cults, because we have based a great deal of our information on the stories of former members, first-person accounts that our critics call "horror-stories."

This very derisive term is used by cult apologists such as Bromley and Shupe to describe the experiences of people who have been involved in these extremist groups. These cult apologists say that individuals who come out of these groups exaggerate their experiences. Former members, according to this perspective, are embarrassed that they were ever associated with such a group. Anticultists convince them that they were involuntarily duped and brainwashed. To explain this embarrassing situation former members recite stories of violence, brainwashing, and manipulation—"horror stories" or "atrocity stories."

Well, I have talked with individuals, many of whom are born-again Christians, who have told me about what I would consider very destructive behavior, including physical abuse. For example, I can think of one young man who told me that as a child growing up in a cult he was forced on occasion to eat dog food off a plate on the floor and was also forced to give details in public as to his masturbation practices. One means of controlling people and keeping them in line in one group I've studied was the regular use of public humiliation, including such things as spitting in a person's face, slapping, and public ridicule. Such practices were common in the People's Temple, for example.

The Children of God regularly engage in religious prostitution—they call it "flirty fishing." They are now encouraging and allegedly teach incest as a doctrine. They also allegedly encourage child-adult sexual relations. I have received the testimonials of some former members because I have never lived with the Children of God in the role of what sociologists call "participant-observer." If I were to officially visit their group, they certainly would not show me, a visiting scholar, some of these activities—especially sexual activities. So the only way I have of getting some kinds of information on some of these groups is through former members. Many of these former members are born-again Christians. I have to either take their word for it and accept the fact that they are telling me the truth, or I have to say that they are distorting the truth and that their reported experiences involving groups such as the Children of God are a product of their rich imagination, made up to cover or explain the mistake they have made by getting into the group in the first place.

Some of my verification of the activities of the Children of God comes from Deborah Davis. Deborah Davis is the daughter of "Moses" Berg, the founder of the movement. She has authored, with her husband, Bill, an excellent book entitled, *The Children of God: The Inside Story* (Zondervan). She was with the movement since its inception in 1968 in Huntington Beach, California. She left voluntarily several years ago.

Many of the people I have interviewed in the course of my research have left voluntarily. This is another disagreement I have with the people who are critical of the anticult movement. They say we get most of our infomation from people who have been deprogrammed. They claim that people who have gone through the deprogramming process have been brainwashed by the deprogrammers. Many of the people I have talked with have not been deprogrammed. They have left cults of their own free will. I agree with Gordon that there is a high turnover in some of these groups and that many people do leave on their own. The people who have exited by choice have not been "contaminated" by the anticultists, by the deprogrammers, or by evangelical Christians. I'm in touch regularly with people who come to me without having had any contact with the so-called anticult movement. Their perception of life in a cult is very similar to those who have been deprogrammed.

So I would ask David Bromley and Anson Shupe, Gordon Melton, and other cult apologists who have written on this topic and who have very low regard for the reports of former members what evaluative terms they would use to describe behavior that involves the sexual abuse of children, physical violence, and other, less visible psychological harm. Gordon says there's little or no evidence for this kind of thing. I disagree with him because I've talked with people who have been there. The daughter of the the founder of the Children of God will tell anyone about her experiences. Her own brother committed suicide because of pressures brought on him by his own father. Deborah Davis will tell anyone that her father has been involved in incest. We've got all kinds of evidence from multiple independent sources to indicate the cults *are* harmful, spiritually and physically.

To be honest, I have a hard time with people who downplay the stories of former members. I'm the first to admit that there are some people who have exaggerated their cult experiences and who have an ax to grind. But what do we do with the vast majority of honest former members who are not exaggerating? The darker side of cults has been largely ignored by those who disapprove of the anticult movement, and I think that's being intellectually dishonest.

I draw a very strong distinction between former members who have been deprogrammed and those who have not. I remember being on a panel with Marsha Rudin in Milwaukee, during which I drew that distinction very sharply. Former members who have not been deprogrammed have been and continue to be my main source for verification of data. If former members who have been deprogrammed and former members who have not been deprogrammed tell me the same story, I'll tend to believe them. That's the technique I think we should highlight. It's very important. *Deprogramming distorts the reports of a person's experience in a cult, especially during the first year or two after the deprogramming.* Deprogramming encourages a single, specific world view and encourages a person to seek justification as a victim rather than responsibility as an adult. Deprogrammers seek to place all the guilt on the group and remove any choice that the individual made in joining the group. That's both incorrect and depersonalizing.

I become especially upset when I hear the testimonies of deprogrammed former members. I see the distortion in their tale when they begin to repeat old stories they heard during the deprogramming as if they were their own experience.

Thus, in summary, I have come to prize the members who left, as do the great majority, of their own will and who have no financial or other vested commitments to the telling of their story.

Then we must say more about physical abuse. Earlier I mentioned a pattern in the physical abuse of children. It tends to occur in aberrant conservative, Bible-believing groups rather than Eastern or occult groups. Again the distinction has to be drawn between members of the group who on their own physically abuse a child and a situation in which the group itself condones abuse. In the case of the House of Judah, the group and the leader condoned the physical abuse that led to the death of the child. That is not necessarily the case in other groups, though they must bear some responsibility in cases where they have created an atmosphere of the acceptance by adults of the physical punishment of children. Accepting physical punishment as normal and proper provides a comfortable atmosphere for child abusers.

Let me make one other comment. I didn't get an answer from Gordon with regard to the statement mentioned earlier in this dialogue from page 40 of his book *The Cult Experience*. Allow me to interject my own name in the quotation: "If [Enroth] has a religious stance [I would say a Christian stance] that assumes a person of another faith is either deluded by false teachers, or inspired by demonic forces, then a negative interpretation of a person's involvement in a religious group that is outside the national religious consensus is guaranteed."

Gordon goes on to say, "This kind of stance, is of course, the standard fare of religious bigotry." Essentially, what Gordon is saying is that I'm a bigot because I think that people like Moon and David Berg are false prophets. I would go so far as to say that the logical extension of his thinking is that the New Testament writers, particularly Paul, would be bigots because they said a great deal about false teachers, false prophets, false teaching. I think they had a lot to say with regard to demonic forces.

So that would be my question. What about those of us who take a Christian stance and do believe in the reality of demonic forces, who do believe that people's minds have been spiritually brainwashed by Satan? Cultists' minds have been darkened by the spiritual forces of darkness that Paul talks about. What's wrong with that kind of stance?

MELTON: I would say it's a dangerous opinion to hold. It's something that can predispose a person to move into a bigoted stance and commit bigoted acts. It can, to be specific, move one to say, "Because the Children of God have done such-and-such an evil thing, then all cults do it." Because one group is bad, everybody we call a cult is bad. We generalize from the particular to the general without sufficient evidence. That's the real problem. Approaching alternative religions from a negative predisposition, as demonic phenomena, the special work of Satan in our generation, while not in itself bigotry, can lead and has led to bigotry.

ENROTH: Well, you need to make that clear. You do not make your position clear, unfortunately.

MELTON: Thank you for bringing it to my attention. I will clarify that point in the next edition.

ENROTH: I agree with what you're saying, that we can't generalize from the Children of God to all cults, but can we not generalize that there is a pattern of evil in all new religious movements?

MELTON: There is a pattern of religious evil, of metaphysical evil. But it is shallow and false theology to see the cults as the central clear embodiment of that evil, as if the churches did not participate and evangelicals were guiltless. Any evil represented by cults and the growing diversity of religion in America pales by comparison to the satanic forces working to create world hunger, leading to political repression, or corrupting the powerful leaders of established institutions.

Also, any pattern of metaphysical evil, heresy, that we as Christians claim to be our main bone of contention with the cults must not be turned into law. Fighting heresy is no excuse for organizing groups and seeking government intervention in the lives of religious groups, even if they are cults. (I was, I must admit, happy that so many evangelicals joined the petitions in favor of the Supreme Court's hearing of Moon's case.) It is dangerous to use heresy, the nature of the evil most evangelicals would identify in a cult, as a basis for social organization.

I don't want my daughter to join a cult. I will call the law on any religious group that breaks the law. But it's dangerous to support special legal measures against today's unpopular religions.

ENROTH: So, rather than merely describe and categorize these movements, I think we need to help Christians to discern.

Again, it comes back to a matter of truth and error. The categories of "true religion" and "false religion" are not popular with traditional academicians. Understandably, they think we are very narrow-minded because we feel that a distinction can be made between truth and error. We would hope that Gordon and others who are both scholars and evangelical Christians would very loudly and clearly articulate in public what I think is a basic evangelical Christian stance vis-à-vis false religions.

With regard to deprogramming, I have a lot of reservations about the practice. There has been some misunderstanding of my views, and some observers have placed me in a camp with the deprogrammers because of an earlier book I wrote called *Youth, Brainwashing, and the Extremist Cults.* Gordon in his review of that book in *Christianity Today* said that I advocated kidnaping cult victims. This is not true, but that was his interpretation and the interpretation of others, largely because I described several deprogrammings that had a "successful" outcome. I've never advocated coercive deprogramming or the use of force in any form in order to retrieve an adult from a cult.

I would simply raise what I think is an important question. How many mainstream evangelicals (Gordon uses the term "Christian leaders") are advocates of deprogramming? I'd like to know the names of those Christian leaders. I'd also like to know which mainstream evangelical cult ministries advocate deprogramming and have participated actively in such activity. I find it difficult to believe that many mainstream evangelicals are active in the deprogramming business. There are selected individuals—evangelicals to be sure—who have had their children deprogrammed. I've talked with some of them. And some of them get very upset with me when I tell them that I don't think deprogramming is the way to go. I tell them, "It's your decision; it can backfire; there can be some very negative repercussions."

However, there are times when I feel I almost have to come to the defense of deprogrammers because of what I see as inflammatory rhetoric with regard to deprogramming by some critics of the practice. I really think that some of what has been written criticizing deprogramming is grossly exaggerated. On the basis of my interviewing of people who have been deprogrammed, I find little support for the assertions of the critics of deprogramming that young people are routinely tortured physically and mentally during deprogramming sessions. Incidentally, for personal and professional reasons I have never witnessed a deprogramming. I admit that there are occasional violent episodes, that some things take place that nobody can countenance.

On the other hand, many of the people I talk to who have gone through deprogramming say that it has been less than violent. The lights haven't been on twenty-four hours a day. They've been allowed to sleep eight hours a night. In fact, they told me that they slept more during the deprogramming than they did most nights when they were in the cult. They report that they've been treated rather well, while at the same time admitting that it is often a very intense experience. I do know of situations in which there has been sexual exploitation.

But my point is that that is clearly the exception rather than the normative experience. In short, I think that those critical of "anticultists" have blown this matter of deprogramming out of proportion.

Let me also share another example of distortion that concerns deprogramming—and here I quote from a paper by Gordon presented at a professional meeting in Cincinnati that is reprinted in part in his book *The Cult Experience*. He says that the return of a deprogrammed person to a normal life is difficult to achieve. "The fact that so many do not or cannot return to a normal existence is strange if we accept the deprogrammer's understanding of what they are doing." Then he does say later on, "Some people do return to normal life."

I would say that, based on my own research experience, *many* people return to normal existence. I think there is clear evidence that people who have been deprogrammed—and I am not here necessarily condoning deprogramming—can and do take normal jobs. They become public school teachers, computer specialists, businessmen and women, etc. A person gets the impression from reading what Gordon and others have written that these people have been through a horrible experience, that their parents have put them through physical and mental torture, and that many awful things happen to them, including commitment to mental hospitals. I say that's ridiculous; it's simply not true. I can submit all kinds of evidence of deprogrammed people who have returned to normal life.

So I'm simply pointing out that the rhetoric on both sides of the fence gets kind of strong. I'm the first to admit that some of the parents that I have had contact with in the so-called anticult movement feel very emotional about some of these issues. Some become crusaders. My point is that the antianticultists also become crusaders and have an ax to grind, professionally and personally. I think social scientists have to be honest enough to admit that there are some people—more than just a few—who have returned to normal life. Most former members become regular, functioning, contributing members of society, and if they experience probems, it is more than likely, in my opinion (and I know that Gordon and I disagree here), due to their cult experience. I'm not a psychiatrist so I can't prove that, but impressionistically I also feel that some of the individuals who have problems adjusting had problems before they went into the cult. Those problems haven't been resolved, and they've even been exacerbated, perhaps, as a result of the cult experience.

I have talked with many people, on the other hand, who have been debilitated by their experience in cultic groups. A former member of one Eastern group—and I have no reason to doubt his word—told me that after meditating for hours and hours every day, his mind became so much jelly beans. He said he lost the ability to balance his checkbook. He could not add and subtract any more. I know that sounds far-fetched and difficult to believe, but I have actually had that kind of experience shared with me many times. And there are people who have had a great deal of difficulty getting back into mainstream society after coming out of cults but who have never been near a deprogrammer. For example, people leaving the Children of God or the Church of the Living Word (of Apostle Stevens) or people coming out of Faith Tabernacle (founded by Eleanor Daries) and other aberrational Christian groups have found reentry to be painful. They have experienced confusion, guilt, and depression. Sometimes it takes months, if not years, for them to go near a church because they have been so emotionally seared by the experience. They can't trust a pastor, they can't trust another religious authority figure.

I disagree with Gordon in that I think there is a high degree of influence, control, and harmful manipulation in cultic organizations. I think it's very, very difficult for individuals who have been in these extremely totalistic communal groups for years to suddenly reverse roles and fit back into conventional society. Such people have difficulty returning to normal life, but eventually they do.

I think there's inflammatory rhetoric on both sides of the deprogramming issue. As a matter of fact, deprogramming isn't taking place very much anymore. Ted Patrick (a well-known deprogrammer) has gotten burned by lawsuits. Parents who once supported him are beginning to see that that's not the best way to fly. At present there is a less controversial methodology being used that is known as "exit counseling." In some ways it is similar to deprogramming, but it usually lacks the coercive dimension. Like the word "cult," the terms "exit counseling" and "deprogramming" mean many things to many people.

The problem is that someone like myself who clearly has come out against deprogramming is nevertheless frequently lumped with the more militant anticultists. I have been threatened, harassed and given a hard time by organizations like APRL, the Alliance for the Preservation of Religious Liberty, an organization made up of people who are supportive of cultic groups. I have been called a "dangerous" person. I have been denounced as someone who is an advocate of deprogramming. I have been labeled an "antireligious" person by organizations purporting to promote freedom of religion. Anyone who dares to make value judgments about minority religions runs the risk of being called "antireligious."

There's a lot of misinformation on both sides, and therefore it's very difficult for the typical parent out there to know what to do and where to go for advice and help. I believe that they often have valid concerns for offspring who are in groups that are potentially harmful. Gordon says, "I have never known deprogrammers to pull someone from the really harmful groups." I would be interested to know which groups he has in mind and which ones he would categorize as "really harmful." When I talk with parents who see a radical change in their children to the extent of suddenly wanting to drop out of the university and wanting to drop out of life, young adults losing weight and becoming physically debilitated, those parents want to do something about it. I can understand sometimes why they would go the route of deprogramming.

Then parents say, "What if it was your child, what would you do, Dr. Enroth?" Well, I'm not sure what I would do. There are *some* parents who have resisted deprogramming and who have patiently waited and prayed for the day that their son or daughter would voluntarily leave a group. I admire their stance, but it's a tough one. Some people do leave cults voluntarily.

One family that I know well has opted against the deprogramming alternative. Their son has been a member of an aberrational Christian group for the last dozen years. For a long time he had cut himself off from his family. His "church" is very cultic, even though it claims to be Christian. It is very totalistic, very controlling, very demanding, very manipulative. I remember several years ago when the young man's mother called me early one morning, all excited. She said, "Ron, last night I talked to my son by phone for the first time in seven years."

That's very tragic. These parents have had their Christmas gifts to their son returned unopened and letters returned unanswered. They tried to maintain some kind of friendly relationship with their son and were repeatedly rebuffed and cast in the role of Satan. But they've never had him deprogrammed. Instead they have prayed and remained hopeful, faithful, and loving. They have sent those Christmas gifts even though they've been returned. I have to commend them for that.

But it's been twelve long years! Recently, this young man came home for the first time for a visit with a friend from his group. His parents erected a big sign in the front yard, "Welcome Home!" It was very moving. And the young man is not out of the group yet. His parents have seen a breakthrough, an answer to prayer. They're waiting for him to leave—in God's time.

But many parents aren't willing to wait twelve years for their son or daughter to come home. They push the panic button and hire the deprogrammer. To say "Be patient and pray" doesn't appeal to a lot of people, especially non-Christians. There is a real tension, a real dilemma. Those of us who are involved with this kind of thing have to sort these issues out and help people to see the pros and cons of the various options open to them. I think we have to be honest and say, "If you decide to go with a deprogrammer, that *could* have negative repercussions. You may totally alienate yourself forever from your son or daughter." On the other hand, parents may feel that the situation is so critical that some form of intervention is necessary. They have to make that decision themselves.

So it's a very sticky business. Deprogramming can mean, as I said before, many things to many people. I know of pastors who have simply talked with members of the Unification Church or other cults, and they have been accused of being deprogrammers. It's that kind of thing I react against. I feel that critics of the parents' organizations have not sufficiently discerned the facts or made the important differentials between coercive deprogramming and other forms of exit counseling that are very often entered into voluntarily. I would really like to be shown the evidence of large numbers of mainstream evangelicals kidnaping people and trying to change their faith in a coercive way. Also, I think the number of mainstream Christians who supposedly have been deprogrammed is grossly exaggerated. The examples that are frequently cited involving Episcopalians, Baptists, and Assemblies of God members are very, very few in reality.

Question: Dr. Melton, you're a Methodist minister and an evangelical Christian. How can you justify doing anything besides trying to defeat non-Christan religions, based on what you believe as a Christian and what you believe as the truth?

MELTON: Taking that approach has, I think, proved non-productive in the end. Trying to defeat the cults has simply not accomplished anything—in large part due to ignorance. The attack upon the cults has to a significant extent been based on lack of information and false or distorted information. My basic ministry to the church, as I see it, is informing people as to what is really out there. I offer this information to the church to use and react to as it encounters the world.

Second, I think that for all of our lifetime certainly, and maybe for some generations to come, we as Christians will have to live in a highly pluralistic situation. On the very practical level, we evangelicals (without giving up any of our affirmations of the gospel) have got to learn to get along with our non-evangelical neighbors. Interreligious strife is not just counterproductive, it is downright hurtful on a social level. Not only do we as Christians have to share the gospel, but *we have to teach our members to live with their neighbors who differ.* If I share the gospel with my neighbor, and she or he nevertheless decides to become a Hindu, I've still got to live with him or her. It's not as if my Hindu neighbor was off in India. He's next door in the apartment. I feel we have a responsibility to spread valid nonpolemical information about various groups so we can learn to live with some degree of peace in the social community. There is a place in the church school to discuss other religions and point out why we feel Christianity is superior to them both individually and collectively. Also, and I speak to my ministerial colleagues particularly at this point, there needs to be time given to simply tell people about other religions and dispel the distrust, fear, and hostility that accompanies the unknown and can result in prejudicial actions toward neighbors that follow a different religion. We need to understand and communicate to our members why people go to the school board and say that we cannot have prayers in the public schools because they are Hindus and a prayer to Christ offends them. I know I would be offended if I had to send my daughter to a school that began each day with a chant to Krishna, and I paid tax money to support it. This example is just one typical problem.

Thus I am suggesting that we have to continue to share the gospel at every opportunity, but we have also to learn to dialogue and understand and develop the ability to relate in a non-derogatory fashion to people we live and work with who are not ready to accept to the gospel just now.

Question: You earlier mentioned your set of standards for evaluating different groups, one secular and one Christian. You said you found these standards hard to handle because you were not a theologian but a church historian. I was wondering what place biblical truth plays in your general writing and speaking about any given group.

MELTON: It's taking on an increasing importance, because I have spent two decades primarily in learning, and I have reached a position where I'm doing more writing and teaching, and I am speaking more to church groups than in the past.

Let me clarify the point about finding difficulty in talking about biblical truth in relation to some groups. I find it fairly easy to talk about biblical standards, for example, in relation to Jehovah's Witnesses or Seventh-Day Adventists or Ultra-dispensationalists—these groups share at least some relationship to the Bible and accept its authority. I find them internally inconsistent and can with some confidence critique them on many grounds from their method of interpreting the Bible to specific misunderstandings of it.

Then I get to the non-Christian groups, and it's a whole new ball game. None of these groups relates to biblical standards. Each has a different holy book, a different theology—and it's not a variation on what I do. Everything, and I mean everything, they do is different. We share very little in common. There are, of course, some points of convergence.

The Buddha taught compassion just as Christ taught love. But the two concepts still vary immensely. No matter the point, wherever you compare Christianity and Hinduism or Buddhism, you've got something different. You are no longer confronting heresy, you are confronting a different religious gestalt.

Question: Earlier you also mentioned Gnostics today. The Colossians in the Bible were faced with an early stage of Gnostic Jewish heresy. You mentioned yet another group, the Arians. Can you distinguish between them?

MELTON: The Arians deny the deity of Christ; the Gnostics deny his humanity.

Question: How then is the person who says "Just Jesus and me" like a Gnostic?

MELTON: The broader implication of Christ's humanity concerns God's entry into the world of matter. From that action (as well as from the whole notion of creation itself) God says that the world is important. On a nature level the material world is important, on a social level society is important. Therefore, when you get a person who calls herself or himself a Christian but denies the importance of action in the world or the importance of life in the Christian community (the church), and says it's basically "me and Jesus," and who goes to "church" because the music is sweet and the choir sings nicely and the preacher speaks fluently, while never encountering the fellowship of believers, that is a form of Gnosticism, or at the very least it's moving in that direction, if it's not already full-blown. As I see it, orthodox Christianity is very much involved in the world, it wars with principalities and powers. Christian life apart from a church community is perverted. The New Testament knows of no such life.

3

IS THERE ANY GOOD IN THE CULTS?

Question: You both mention that people go into cults because they're attracted to their authority. Does that suggest that perhaps this is because there's been a vacuum of authority in their homes, or that in the churches we have relinquished authority that we ought to have in the proper sense? Also, does that have any impact on the relinquishing of the authority of the scriptures? Are people seeking an authoritative word, and if we as parents relinquish authority and as a church relinquish a rightful authority, if we as biblical believers begin to relinquish something of the authority of the scriptures, does that invite people to go out and seek authority figures in other places?

ENROTH: I think so, very definitely. I feel that there is something of an authority vacuum in our society, and I think it in part relates to our family structure as well as to the church. There are lots of people out there looking for this sense of authority. Some of the young adults who get involved in these groups relate to cult leaders, especially masculine cult leaders, as parent figures. The cult becomes a surrogate family for them. Frequently, but not always, there is some problem at home with family dynamics—communication difficulties with parents, etc. Several preliminary studies have indicated that kind of situation. Very often there is a weak or absent father—not always, but frequently that's the case. And it's been interesting to me that many of the former cult members I've talked to, whether they were deprogrammed or left voluntarily, have fathers whose occupations are technically or scientifically oriented—physicians, engineers, especially. There appears to be something of a pattern—a distant relationship with the father.

Also related to this erosion of authority is what I see as a shift in our society away from the predominant Judeo-Christian tradition. Gordon and I agree that the intrusion of the new religions, especially Eastern religions, is something new for our society. There is not the same common religious base that was accepted for years in our society. Things are open, up for grabs. Young people do not have this Judeo-Christian base by which to evaluate things. Therefore we have an increasingly theologically or religiously naive public. They are vulnerable to almost any guru who comes down the pike. They do not have the ability to ask the right questions of new religious leaders. Therefore a vacuum exists, and into that vacuum come the new religious movements. Not a surprising development.

Question: Does that suggest the cult leader or the cult itself becomes a surrogate authority figure in place of God?

ENROTH: Yes. In one of my books I make the statement that a god in the flesh is easier for some people to believe in. There are some individuals who can identify more readily with a living teacher, master, guru, or whatever. They can see him, touch him, talk with him.

I remember being at the Unification Seminary in New York for a day a couple of years ago. Moon wasn't there that particular morning, but the word got around that he was coming to campus later that day. I was there as one of five authors invited by the Moonies to be their guests. We all had heard the rumor that "Father" might be visiting the campus that afternoon. Those of us who were visitors went to the main entrance of the seminary and there joined all the seminary students, staff, and faculty to await Moon's arrival. I wish I had a photograph to preserve the expressions on the faces of those Moonies—the sense of expectation—Master, Leader, Father was coming, "god" in the flesh. There was tremendous anticipation. It turned out that Moon wasn't in the limosine. His driver got out and said that "Father" had decided to go fishing and that he wasn't going to come to campus. He supposedly needed to be alone and wanted to meditate. There was such a letdown as they all went their various ways.

That attitude of adoration is evident even in the groups that don't necessarily view their leader as divine. However, in the Eastern religious groups the leader or guru is often felt to be a "realized" being, which thereby elevates him or her to deity.

And, although I'm reluctant to invoke Jonestown and the People's Temple, that's of course what happened with Jim Jones. He eventually displaced God. We see the same kind of frightening devotion and loyalty being given contemporary gurus like Rajneesh and Moon.

MELTON: We found in our survey data on new religions that as high as 80 to 85 percent of the people who join alternative religions come from nominally religious homes. That is true of Jewish as well as Christian homes. Very few cult members report ever having been active in their church or synagogue, though 90 percent report that their parents were members.

This observation was born out most graphically in a recent survey in the Witchcraft community of Georgia. I can still remember Rodney Stark, who did the computer work on the survey for the Institute, calling me on the phone all the way from Seattle when he got the printout.

He began, "Gordon, there won't be but one surprise in the data."

I said, "What's that?" He replied, "There are no Baptists."

Now Georgia is 50 percent Baptist, and the Witches-

Pagans were drawing pretty equally from all of the other religious groups in the area. But there were no Baptists. Part of that lack could be accounted for racially. The black community is heavily Baptist, while the Wiccan community is almost totally white. But still, Baptists who grow up in the church do not filter toward the cults.

This finding harks back to the authority question. In many homes, even nominally religious ones, there exists no religious authority. In some cases there is no religion at all, in spite of church membership. The new religions supply religion and religious authority to people who only experienced it before as something someone else talks about. For many it is their first real encounter with religion. They have been shopping around the "cults." Usually they have been to two groups before they find the one they eventually join. Interesting data.

ENROTH: I agee. I think, for example, that in the Jewish community you wouldn't find an orthodox Jewish person getting caught up in these groups. The cultural or ethnic Jew is more likely to get involved. That's been my experience, too, with the Catholic and Protestant community. Nominal Christians are more vulnerable. In fact, I had a former member of the Children of God tell me that they did not bother to try to convert pious Catholics, Mormons, or evangelical Christians. They weren't worth the time. He tried to identify those persons with a very nominal religious background and pursue them.

MELTON: The "aberrant" Christian groups that you've been studying do go after evangelicals, young Christians especially. But all the groups that have been around for a decade know the scene. They know that there are some types of people that are not worth their time trying to recruit.

ENROTH: Certain kinds of what I term "aberrational Christian" groups definitely would have some attraction for some evangelicals—The Way, The Walk, Hobart Freeman's Faith Assembly, plus the "shepherding" kinds of ministries that are increasingly popular. One such group—little known outside its immediate locale but typical of many groups springing up across the nation—the Community Chapel and Bible Training

Center in Seattle, is pastored by Donald Barnett, a non-Trinitarian pentecostal who disavows identification with the shepherding movement but who nevertheless exercises firm control over his flock. Former members report experiencing spiritual and psychological bondage while in the group. The exit process is painful since the leaders ban all contact with "dissidents" who are said to have a "spirit of rebellion." Contact with other Christian groups is minimal, great emphasis is given to visions and other subjective experiences, there is a preoccupation with demons and a feeling that the church is being persecuted by other, less spiritual Christians. These characteristics are common to many groups on the margins of evangelicalism that, in my opinion, exhibit some cultic tendencies.

Question: Why would evangelicals go to those groups and not to the Moonies? What do they have to offer?

MELTON: Their deviancy level is lower. You can join The Way, for example, and you can think of yourself as an evangelical Christian. You don't have to shave your head, change your name, wear weird clothing, read strange books. You avoid the social ostracism of a Hare Krishna or member of the Sikh Dharma. You are a bit different, but you have been taught that evangelical Christians should have standards that are a little different from the world's.

ENROTH: These marginal groups are much more intense, too, much more subjective, more feeling oriented; and they're into a form of discipleship that some of us might view as extreme but that obviously meets the needs of some Christians who feel a deficiency in mainstream evangelical churches. They stress a form of commitment and a degree of involvement that is sometimes sadly lacking in mainstream churches. In other words, there *are* some positive aspects to membership in such groups. The problem is that too many sincere seekers end up in groups without checks and balances, in groups that tend to go off the deep end. Donald Mackay, the former president of Princeton Seminary, has said, "Commitment without reflection

is fanaticism in action." So we find some Christians really wanting the kind of commitment that they don't find in the Baptist
church, in the Presbyterian church, but they find it in group X,
Y, or Z. They find it in these groups that are very spiritually ex-
clusive, very down on the traditional churches, and very
control-oriented.

Question: So would you say these people are trying to move
toward God?

ENROTH: I would say regardless of whether it's an aberrational Christian group or an Eastern group or a self-
improvement group that we're talking about, we have to first
of all affirm the spiritual search. Obviously, they are looking
for a measure of reality, truth, and spiritual experience. We
must as Christians affirm that search. We may not agree with
what they ultimately will achieve in terms of membership in
these groups and the "truth" that they receive. What I try to tell
parents is that, as difficult as it may be for you to accept your
child's involvement in this particular group, you've got to
realize that your son or daughter is feeling a spiritual lack of
some kind that is very real to them at this point in life.

I think, too, that those who get involved in aberrational
Christian groups are looking for something better, something
more exciting—the perfect church, the perfect pastor. It's easy
to find faults with more conventional churches. Whatever the
nature of the group, there are people who go from teacher to
teacher, guru to guru, group to group, experience to experience, looking for that perfect teacher, that perfect guru, that
perfect "spiritual master." They become spiritual butterflies.

MELTON: I find that, and I also find the person who has
had a bad experience as a teen-ager in traditional churches, in
the church in which she or he was raised. I see this over and
over again. Around Chicago it's primarily Roman Catholic
priests that have been insensitive or not present when needed.
That insensitivity has driven the young person from the church.
Add to the experience of an insensitive pastor a youth spent in

a church that believes it is the "only" church. If you leave the Worldwide Church of God or, until recently, the Roman Catholic Church, it is very hard for you to go to any other church, even in your embittered state. So you go to something that is not Christian at all.

But let's intensify the problem on the larger scale. Half the people in the United States are raised pretty much as secularists. That's fifty percent of the young adults who have had little or no real religious background. Colleges are a real smorgasbord. So if you have been raised as a secularist, when you go to a college or university you become religiously open. You are ready to adopt a religious commitment of some kind. In the smorgasboard you can find one you like, and one that likes you.

When you are in the seeker situation and you encounter a new group (except where the deviancy question gets to be important), the teachings of the group are not nearly as important as the fellowship within the group. Anyone who has been in any of the Eastern groups can tell you of the warm friendship he or she found. You may call it lovebombing, but that is a poor metaphor—it's real fellowship, real closeness. And if you had previously been in a big thousand-member church and you didn't know half the people you worshiped with on Sunday morning, the contrast is startling. You move from a situation in which you cannot even call the members by name into an intimate group that is very supportive of you personally.

ENROTH: I agree very strongly. One of the things I always tell audiences regarding the matter of joining a cult is that the doctrinal or belief system of any given cult is almost always a secondary factor in the decision to sign on. The primary reasons that people are attracted to cults are social in nature. People join cultic groups because they meet very real human needs. Potential converts—whether to new religious movements (like the Unification Church) or to older, more established cults (like the Mormons)—are attracted to what they perceive to be nice, friendly people who seem to care for them and affirm them as worthwhile individuals. They are attracted to the sense of family, the sense of community, the sense of purpose that these groups capitalize on.

The average converts don't join the Latter-day Saints, for example, because they discovered an exciting book called the *Book of Mormon*. Likewise, the young person who joins the Moonies rarely does so because he or she was introduced to a book entitled *Divine Principle*. People are attracted to Mormonism because of that group's image of wholesomeness, clean-cut Americanism, and concern for family values. Young adults are drawn to the Moonies because the recruiters they meet seem to be sincere, committed, and excited about their group. Doctrinal considerations are overshadowed by personal considerations. Indoctrination into the teachings of the group comes later.

This all has implications for the way that many evangelical Christians approach the topic of cults. We traditionally have emphasized doctrinal differences and distinctives. We are taught: the Mormons believe this, the Bible teaches otherwise. The Moonies teach thus and so; Bible believing Christians believe otherwise. Don't misunderstand me—that kind of information is crucial. It's basic to discerning truth from error. However, evangelicals need to recognize that factors other than doctrinal or theological concerns are, initially at least, of primary significance to cult converts. We must learn to look at the whole spectrum of variables that are a part of the decision to join a cult—including psychological, sociological, and personal needs.

MELTON: At this point you have to make some decisions, for by the time you reach college, the blank slate no longer exists. But if the choice was put to you, would you rather have a secular humanist next door or a Moonie or a Hare Krishna or a member of The Way International? That is a very real choice for some people.

Among the people who join one of the cults, nine out of ten will leave the group within two years. That's the turnover rate at present. We have counted some thirty to thirty-five thousand people who have become members of the Unification Church, but there are only five thousand of them around today. Approximately thirty thousand came and went pretty quickly. But five thousand remain in the church. Some individuals, one in ten, will stick with a new group for the rest of their lives or at least a significant period of it. Is that good or bad? We have to say that we would rather they be evangelical Christians; I would certainly like to see them use all that zeal and energy and commitment in the cause of Christ. But if the choice were between their being Moonies or secular humanists (i.e., completely irreligious), the choice is not so clear. Which would you choose? I'd rather have the Moonie. I hasten to add that there are some groups (ECKANKAR, the Children of God/Family of Love, Church of Satan) I would not say that about; but I would rather a person be a Buddhist than a secularist. At least with the Buddhist there's a sense of the sacredness of life, an appreciation of a holy realm. Especially when it comes to participation in the political process, to the making of public policy, I would much rather have people in positions of power and in the voting booth who treat life as sacred than those who have a purely materialistic, mundane view of the world.

ENROTH: I would like to comment further on the question of the possible benefits in the cults. There are some people who claim they became better persons as a result of some of their experiences in a structured group. I can think of a person who was in an aberrational Christian group for several years. She said she was a very quiet, insecure, withdrawn person when she first joined. But because of the nature of the group and the fact that they were forced to give public witness, she acquired a measure of self-confidence and an ability to speak in public as a result of her membership. She considers that an unexpected benefit, although the negative far outweighed any positive dimensions.

I think too that there is a real sense of family and community and comradeship that can be viewed as a positive experience while in a cultic group. Whether misdirected or not, there is the sense of being part of a group that is doing something of eternal significance. It all gets back to the principle that cults are successful because they are meeting basic human needs. Unless we realize that, we are overlooking an important part of the phenomenon. How they meet those needs and how they spell out their truth claims is, of course, a matter of controversy.

Question: Gordon, you said before that the cults lose a lot of people and that former members often become evangelical Christians after this first religious experience . . . .

MELTON: At this time all our observations amount to anecdotal material. We have almost no data on what happens to people when they leave the cults. In some cases we know they go to other religious groups—they show up in the surveys of the groups they then join.

But I have worked with people, and I could think of a handful just off the top of my head, who have gone into groups after a childhood in a church, spent a couple of years as a devotee or premie (almost like two years in the army), came out more or less bitter, and after a while found their way back to their home church. Two years further down the line they reported to me that they had learned a lot in the cult, and that it was a growing experience, but they have now found something to live for, a real commitment for their life.

Question: Do you have any data on that, Ron?

ENROTH: No. I would have similar impressionistic conclusions. But I really don't know. I think some of them get burned out and drop out of religion completely. Some of those probably eventually come back, others do not. I talked to a girl recently who has become an atheist, she said, as a result of being burned in a particular group. But we really don't have firm data; it's an area to be researched.

MELTON: It would be mighty hard to research.

Question: We were talking before about authority figures. . . . Is there a sense in which all people have a deep-seated need for commitment to someone or something important? And have you sensed strains of deep commitment in the cult experience?

ENROTH: I would say definitely yes . . . . One of the questions reporters frequently ask me is, "Are cult leaders sincere? Do they really believe what they are teaching, or are they Elmer Gantry types—charlatans, con artists?" I believe they are sincere. I think that Moon believes he's the Messiah, and I think most cult leaders (and followers) are very committed and they are not charlatans. At the same time I think that they do use, either consciously or unconsciously, techniques that are less than laudatory to control and manipulate people. They are on a power trip. That quest for power is combined with a holy cause that usually involves a sincere attempt to save young people or the world. So I don't think they are charlatans in the sense that they don't really believe what they are preaching. However, although I think they are sincere, I think they are sincerely *wrong.*

Again, we have to affirm the search of young people for commitment, for idealistic goals. The people who get involved in these groups are highly idealistic—they really do want to change the world. I have often said that I'd like to have the Moonies that I've met in my classes and in my church. They are very fine people. Because I am a critic of the cults, I want to make sure that I'm heard on this point. If you read David Bromley and Anson Shupe, Tom Robbins, and even Gordon Melton —in short, writers who have described the "anticultists"—you get the impression that the only Moonies that the critics are talking about are the ones who are "zonked," brainwashed to the point that they can't communicate, emotional vegetables. That is an unfair characterization of our depiction of Moonies. There are no doubt some Moonies who are like that. There are probably some evangelicals that are that way too.

But for the most part, I do sense commitment, loyalty, and a genuine feeling about spiritual issues. I remember talking to some Moonie missionaries who were given the job of trying to convert ministers and people like myself in Southern California. They spent many hours with us, and we shared with them openly and clearly for a long period of time our view of Scripture and many other issues. And we also shared personally about our relationship with Christ. The Moonies were in tears half way through the three hours that we spent with them, and those were genuine tears, I think. They said, "You are very spiritual people"—and they really meant that. They seemed to resonate with our concern for things spiritual.

And yet I could see after three hours of going around and around with them that we came right back to square one. They seemingly were agreeing with us in some of our critique of the Moonie theology, and I believe they could see where we were coming from, but there was no way they could buy it. We really had not made a dent in their thinking.

This is a frustrating dimension of trying to witness to any cultist. In a real sense, the Moonies are "indoctrinated"—just as the Mormons are indoctrinated. Many Christians have had experiences with Mormons and Jehovah's Witnesses. They are very committed to their teachings, and it's frustrating to try to penetrate those kinds of mental fences.

So I don't think it's a superficial thing at all. I think for the most part they're very committed people. That's why it is difficult to reach them, because you have to show them in love that they are committed to the wrong doctrine, the wrong person, the wrong movement or set of ideals. As one girl told me after two hours of low-key discussion, "You have destroyed everything that I value and cherish in this world. Everything that's important and precious to me you've wiped out." In what I thought was a nonconfrontational approach, I had merely compared the gospel to what she had been taught. She turned to her mother, who had brought her to my office, and said, "I don't want to spend anymore time talking to this guy. He's not helping me or anybody else." She was angry and stormed out of the office. Several weeks later she left The Way International. She told us later that as a result of that discussion she started to think about things she had never considered before. It really angered her because I had raised some points that she had never considered. And in that nonconfrontational way, the wheels started to turn and eventually she left on her own. That's the ideal form of deprogramming. Secular academicians who are cult observers have real problems with that kind of anecdote simply because I use such categories as "right" doctrine and "wrong" doctrine. But for the Christian, such issues are crucial.

MELTON: I know that in the general course of my research I try to build good relationships with the people I meet in various groups. I let them know I am a minister as well as a historian and indicate my availability if they need someone outside of the group to talk to. I go to many conferences sponsored by different groups as an observer only to find myself doing a lot of counseling during portions of the gathering. I believe that we have to be open and ready to offer members of such groups what they have found in the groups that has been so important to them.

Question: Is there a real sense, then, in which these people are finding something vital to them that we simply have failed to give them—love, authority, a place for valid commitment?

MELTON: I believe there are two or three things that an alternative group offers. It offers a place for teen-age expression of commitment. At least in my church, the United Methodist Church, one of the hardest things for the church to deal with is a teen-ager who is really committed to Jesus. We all know how immaturely that commitment can be expressed. A committed teen-ager has a tough time. A person really committed to Jesus wouldn't fit in the average youth group. She or he would want to do different things than what the youth group is likely to be doing. The congregation wouldn't know how to let him or her testify on Sunday morning to what has happened in his or her life. If one of my teen-agers walked into my study and said, "I met Jesus last night and really committed myself to him. I'd like to tell the congregation about it on Sunday," I'm not sure how I would be able to handle that in the context of a mainline Christian denomination.

Yet these "cults" could. They do best with people moving from adolescense to adulthood. They work with them best, and that's what we do worst in the mainline churches.

Second, cults provide a sense of community in contrast to that large impersonal church on the corner. I consider myself an evangelical. I move in liberal Protestant circles where there's much more contrast than with strictly evangelical congregations. Your local United Church of Christ, Presbyterian, or Methodist congregation is more stale and secular than your local Baptist or Pentecostal church is. It's more of a problem in liberal Protestant churches, but that's where most of the members are, at least at present.

ENROTH: I would agree that cultic groups are usually out there where people are hurting—on the campus, or in the community, on the streets. Usually it's the more fundamentalistic or more charismatically oriented groups in evangelicalism that are doing equivalent kinds of ministries. In other words, I don't think it's realistic to expect a young adult to walk in off the streets to the office of First Presbyterian Church or First Baptist Church to seek help, whereas on campus or in another context it's quite likely they'll run into one of these groups and be invited to a seminar or dinner or whatever. That can be a lesson to the church. We need to strengthen our campus ministry and somehow begin to penetrate the hurting society that's really out there and not expect them to come to us.

MELTON: Also remember the second place where groups grow. If you map out an urban area pinpointing all the new religions' congregations, you'll find them in two places—in a circle around university campuses and in the young adult-singles-high school-dropout communities. In Chicago, for example, you find the new religions on the North Side near Belmont and Clark Streets, in New Town and Old Town where many singles live. Then, you find them in Evanston and Rogers Park near Northwestern University and on the Southside near the University of Chicago complex.

ENROTH: Another thing I would observe in this regard

concerns evangelical Christians, including students at Christian colleges, who are attracted specifically to the aberrational Christian groups. These people find such groups appealing because they sense a lack of the experiential in their own faith and in their churches. They lack the subjective experience that is so important to them, and, of course, this need can be and often is exploited in some of these marginal groups. There is also a sense of drama and vitality about their Christian faith missing, and they are attracted to a group like the Church of the Living Word because they sense a dynamism in the services and in the fellowship of this group. Things are happening—it is exciting! It reminds me of the entertainer Flip Wilson, who used to have a stock character called Rev. LeRoy, pastor of the "Church of What's Happening Now." That's exactly the name of the game for some of these experientially oriented aberrational groups. Would-be converts define their Baptist, Methodist, Presbyterian churches as stale, dry, meaningless. Nice people, but wow, they're not really excited about their faith, whereas at this church, when the apostle comes, and he lays hands on people, things happen. Every service is different. I suppose the same kind of appeal can be seen in some mainstream Pentecostal churches. The services are a little different, perhaps more emotional. In some more conventional evangelical churches the young Christian or the dissatisfied, disenchanted young adult doesn't see the dynamic aspects of the Christian faith, and he or she does see it in these other groups. These young adults don't stop to ask important questions and are less discerning along doctrinal lines. More than likely they would reject a concern for doctrine in the first place. "If it feels good, do it."

MELTON: In observing the leadership of both occult and Eastern groups we further found a very high incidence of spontaneous psychic experiences in childhood. They were drawn to the group because it was the first group that listened to their account of a psychic event, tried to explain it, and assisted them to integrate it into their total life.

Question: Gordon, discuss the issue of the psychic more.

Perhaps you could come out with a statement about the psychic and Ron could react.

MELTON: It is both a detailed and an emotional issue. I'm not sure I could cover it adequately in a few minutes, but I'll try. I got involved with the psychic community in the late 1960s. Basically I was doing some research that included Spiritual Frontiers Fellowship (SFF). I found that the easiest way to complete the research with the least hassles was to join. So I gave them fifteen dollars and became a member. I was going through a spiritual crisis myself at the time and through my involvement in Spiritual Frontiers and the ministry provided me by several of the ministers who were active leaders I was led back to a vital faith and a new appreciation of the Bible. During those early years I also began a longtime period of research on the claims of parapsychology, the psychic community, and the biblical evaluation of what today we call the psychic and occult. (We have to remember that the terms psychic and occult, as we use them today, were not used in the Bible. They are rather new ways of discussing paranormal events.)

The bottom line is that what we call the "psychic" (as opposed to the occult), that is, the realm of paranormal experiences, is a natural part of us. Theologically stated, it is a given of creation. There is a part of each of us that responds beyond the five senses in different ways. The Gallup poll points out that twenty-five percent of the general public feels that it has had direct contact with a person who has died. Sixty to seventy percent claim some kind of significant psychic experience, an experience that has been life-changing for them but that has rarely been recounted to anyone else.

I found that such experiences had been a part of my life. I also found that in examining the Scriptures, paranormal experiences had been a part of the life of our biblical heroes, part of the early church. Experience beyond the mundane sphere of accepted phenomena was common to the early church. When a people were gifted in being a focus for healing or could foretell the future, their gifts were called *charismata* and sanctified and put to use as gifts of the Holy Spirit (which they were). In deny-ing those very natural abilities, which some people possess in a strong way, we suppress a very important part of ourselves, a part that can directly relate to the depth of our spirituality and our spiritual growth.

Question: What are some of the things in the Bible that you would see as psychic phenomena?

MELTON: A good, clear, unambiguous example of a biblical event that if it occurred today and was observed by an outsider would be called "psychic" or "paranormal" would be Samuel's seership. In 1 Samuel 9 Samuel is asked to locate the lost donkeys of Jesse, which by the end of the story he does.

However, the purest case of the use of what today we would call the psychic or paranormal is in 1 Corinthians 12— the gifts of the Spirit. If we look at the gifts enumerated there and look at their occurrence today, we would see them both as psychic events. Parapsychologists have a set of technical termi-nology to label each of the gifts—prophecy (precognition), knowledge (clairvoyance), healing (psychokinetic healing), etc. The ability to see into the future, to know things without prior knowledge by the five senses, to act as a focus for healing— these are all abilities shown by people who call themselves Christians, who call themselves Buddhists, Hindus, or Jews, or who profess no religion at all. But when these things are done in the church under the aegis of the Christian community and for its benefit, they become sanctified (holy), and we properly see them as a gift of the Spirit to the church for its growth, exam-ple, and uplift.

The early church, of course, did some things I am not too sure about. I'm not sure I want to chose church leaders by divination, as the church choose the thirteenth Apostle (Acts 1). Casting lots was a very popular form of divination in the first century.The church gave at least passive approval to astrology (in contradiction to the Old Testament denunciations of it). Note the first event to be recorded in the New Testament. The first people to worship Jesus as Lord were three astrologers who found their way to him by following a star, i.e., through their astrological observations.

The people who saw the early church perceived its paranormal life, and that is why we see the confusion recorded in the book of Acts. People in the first century had trouble distinguishing between magicians and the early church leaders. People looked at both and they seemed to be doing the same thing. The book of Acts is, in part, an attempt by the early church to distinguish itself from others who appeared to be similar.

ENROTH: There is a difference between the spiritual gifts and Simon Magus. There was a difference, and you're saying there is no difference. I think what you're saying is very unorthodox.

MELTON: Hear me clearly, Ron. There is a difference between the church and Simon Magus. But remember, no one in the first century talked about the psychic. That's a modern word to indiscriminately describe paranormal events. The difference was not between the psychic and the nonpsychic. Both the early church and Simon Magus were doing things today we would all agree would be extraordinary, paranormal, even miraculous (though I don't like that term). The difference is that the church took normal psychic abilities, the normal abilities that people had, and put them under the discipline of the church, the demands of God, and judged them by their effect on the church and their production of fruitful Christians. Simon Magus's abilities were operating in a completely different context.

The gifts of the Spirit are not limited to the manifestation of extraordinary "psychic" feats; they are normal, natural abilities like teaching, preaching, pastoring, healing, prophesying, speaking in tongues taken into the life of the Christian community, disciplined by its order (1 Cor. 12, 14) and used to its edification. Many people can teach, it's a normal ability. In the church it becomes a gift of the Spirit. Likewise, many people can speak in tongues, but used judiciously in the church such abilities can edify and build up the Body of Christ. That's the difference. Simon Magus had no such godly controls and opened himself to the full range of ungodly influences.

I must admit I am still growing and learning on this point. There are some things that happened in the early church I would find difficult to accept if they began to happen today— calling blindness upon someone, for example. That's what we call black magic today. And at some points it is hard to tell the difference between events that occur inside the church with its approval, and those outside. Though I do not share Kurt Koch's negative opinion of Oral Roberts and Kathryn Kuhlman, I do agree with him that there is little or no difference in what they did and what most Spiritualist healers do.

ENROTH: I disagree tremendously. In other words, you would say that the ability of the Indian guru Sai Baba to heal people is no different from the biblical gift of healing. I personally think that the source of his power to heal people does not come from the God of the universe but comes from the powers of darkness that Scripture states originated with Satan. Satan has power to heal. That's why we use the term "counterfeit" gift. You see no distinction between Sai Baba and Oral Roberts?

MELTON: I see no substantive distinction in that both Sai Baba and Roberts are natural foci for paranormal healing. Both heal people within the range of their abilities, abilities given to them in God's creation. However, Roberts has placed his abilities under the church and is putting it to work there, just as you have put your teaching ability to work under the discipline of the church and use it to serve the church. Sai Baba has his own movement, an offshoot of Hinduism. His gift serves what theologically we both evaluate as a false religion. Swami Vivekananda, like you, had a teaching gift. It's the same native ability. But unlike you, he put it to service in the cause of Hinduism. Both Roberts and Sai Baba heal. Both you and Vivekananda teach. The distinction between you and Vivekananda is the same distinction that exists between Sai Baba and Roberts and the early church and Simon Magus.

ENROTH: I disagree—I do not think that psychic gifting is a normal kind of phenomenon that's resident in all of us.

There is a distinction between the gifts of God's Holy Spirit and what I would call the counterfeit gifts or the counterfeit miracles that are performed by people who are empowered by Satan and his emissaries. There's real power there, and it is difficult for many people to discern the difference. They certainly experience some extraordinary things in some of these movements. They see powers attributed to Moon, for example, including perhaps clairaudience and some of the other so-called psychic phenomena, and they view it as benign, or some kind of natural gift, or as a gift from God.

Frequently in the psychic/occult literature there is reference to healings, to what we would call the miraculous or the supernatural. You also see discussion of this phenomenon in the academic discipline of cultural anthropology. Consider the shaman and medicine men; they certainly heal people. Things do happen. Is that by chance, or is it human power? No, when we look at the New Testament evidences of supernaturalism, that power comes from one of two sources: God the Holy Spirit, or Satan, and not from some human power.

We may disagree here. I do not think it is a human power that can be tapped, although that is the message of many of today's New Age groups. It is also the focus of much Eastern/occult mysticism—the notion that we are in fact divine and therefore have unlimited potential. Self-realization—self with a capital "S"—means to become aware of the divine within, and therefore if we can master spiritual technology (like meditation) in order to become aware of this divine within, we can do anything. The human potential movement with its emphasis on "transformation," is a logical extension of the basic Eastern/occult philosophy that says that people are capable of achieving whatever they wish. We are the masters of our own fate. The message of gurus like Muktananda is: "Heal yourself, kneel to yourself, worship yourself because the true inner Self is divine."

Therefore, healings and other so-called psychic phenomena that take place outside of the context of biblical Christianity are evidences of satanic counterfeiting. I think that perspective is probably more typical of the mainstream evangelical stance.

MELTON: Quite correct. I work out of the context that "what is apart from faith is sin." The demonic is much broader in scope than just the operation of psychic gifts outside of the church.

To back up, I definitely do not want to identify myself with Eastern thought at this point, and would want to separate myself from any kind of deification of the self, even the higher self that goes on in occult circles. Such deification is quite distinct from the Christlikeness we are to assume.

No, what I am saying is (and we may have to wait for a later agreement as we both receive greater understanding) that just as we can touch, feel, and see, we also possess the ability to perceive things beyond the five senses, and we have psychokinetic ability (i.e., the ability to effect the material world with our mind). Such abilities are a natural part of us, given to us by God in creation. Just as we can pervert our recognized abilities and put them to demonic use, we can pervert our paranormal abilities and allow them to be subverted by the demonic

I arrived at this position after many hours of observing Pentecostal meetings, attending various New Age and Spiritualist services, and studying my Bible to try to perceive what was happening in the church in Corinth and Rome and Asia Minor. I have read the books of John W. Montgomery, Kurt Koch and J. Stafford Wright, the finest evangelical writers on the psychic and paranormal. I have studied parapsychology, the dull kind in journals. What began to put it all together for me was a study of the spiritual gifts that I prepared for a Bible study workshop.

Going through the New Testament, I made a list of all the things that were called gifts of the Spirit, either directly or by implication. The list of twenty-plus items included rather mundane things such as teaching, administration, pastoring, visiting the sick. There was nothing rather spectacular, "supernatural" if you wish, about those items. Some people happened to be gifted with those talents. Paul was a talented missionary. Agabus was a gifted prophet (i.e., he could see the future). Some people can stand up and really preach. They were gifted from birth.

Question: Can't that be seen as supernatural from the Christian or biblical perspective?

MELTON: Sure, and that's what I came to see. It's all super-natural. The most mundane is supernatural. The ability of a lay person to visit shut-ins and convey God's concern for them is just as supernatural as someone being healed of cancer at Oral Roberts' prayer meetings. The ability to effectively administer a congregation is just as supernatural a gift as seeing into the future. The ability to lead a youth group is just as much the direct work of the Holy Spirit as speaking in tongues—and I might add just as mundane.

I would say that Christians have to take their abilities, use them in the context of the Christian community, allow them to be disciplined by the church, and most importantly allow them to be judged by the fruits of the Spirit they produce. That has been my continual message. You judge the gifts, primarily, by the fruits, and if the fruits are not there, there is something wrong with the way you are using the gifts.

ENROTH: Let's pursue this a bit further, as well as your association with the Spiritual Frontiers Fellowship (SFF), an organization of ministers who are interested in psychic/occult phenomena. I hear what you're saying about psychic gifts, but I would have difficulty using the word "psychic" as you do because of what it connotes to the average person, including the average evangelical Christian. I could not agree, for exam-ple, with the assertion that there's an astrological bent or a divination dimension in the New Testament. Both astrology and divination are clearly proscribed by many Old Testament passages. God views these practices as "abominations." There are injunctions against fortune-telling, necromancy (contact with the spirit of the dead), and other forms of spiritism. We are enjoined to trust God for our future, not the stars. Astrological charts should not be the source of our business or personal deci-sions. When most people think of astrology, they think of these kinds of matters. There is much more to the realm of "astral religion" than horoscopes, however, and most people are unaware of the possible negative consequences of opening themselves up to the psychic realm.

But moving beyond the specific area of astrology, let's discuss your involvement with the SFF. You have stated that some people discovered a new depth of faith as a result of their association with the Spiritual Frontiers Fellowship. Those of us who are familiar with SFF literature have problems with a statement like that. Articles in SFF publications discuss in a positive, supportive way such topics as seances, communication with the dead, kundalini yoga, the Course in Miracles, and other forms of psychic/occult phenomena—all of which would be viewed with disapproval by the vast majority of evangelical Christians. Your own articles in *Spiritual Frontiers* and *Fate* magazines are favorably disposed toward psychic/occult behavior. I would like to ask you: How has your faith been strengthened and deepened by your involvement with SFF, an organization that is defined by most evangelical Christians as an obviously occult/psychic organization that seems so far removed from the gospel of Jesus Christ and the testimony of his apostles?

MELTON: My experience in SFF occurred at a point of intense spiritual crisis in my life. During my seminary days I had become deeply affected by the death-of-God theology. In fact I could say that the reality of God in my life was missing, and the cultural phenomena described by William Hamilton (as the loss of the experience of God in Western culture) paralleled my personal pilgrimage. The practice of meditative prayer, which I learned in SFF, became a tool to reestablish my contact with God. For that alone I was and still am very grateful. SFF also caused me to do a lot of study of Scripture about things of which I was then only minutely aware. Thus I gained a new and deeper relation with God and a new appreciation of Scripture.

After that point, I found room in SFF and felt that I could stay in it without compromising my faith, because SFF has had a position as a forum group, a position clearly stated on all its literature, for many years. That is, SFF is a place where a lot of different ideas and opinions can be discussed back and forth. For example, I had written one article on kundalini. My article

attacked another article that had identified some of the experiences of the great Christian mystics as kundalini experiences. I wrote what in hindsight was a diatribe, saying that
it was very illegitimate to try to force the accounts of St.
Theresa of Avila and John of the Cross into Hindu kundalini experiences.

Also, at the top of SFF there was a group of pastors—some
Methodists, some Episcopalians—with whom I had a great deal
of fellowship. They, like me, had found, usually in one religious practice (for me it was meditative prayer, for others it is
spiritual healing or receiving some evidence of life after death)
an experience that led them to a deepening or renewal of faith.

Several years after I joined SFF, I was invited to join the
staff. I became SFF's main in-house teacher for several years. I
was happy for the chance to teach in that context and am happy
to note, in reviewing the material after almost a decade, that I
can still stand by it basically. It seems to be biblically and
theologically sound.

SFF is an open-membership organization. Anyone can join
for a few dollars. And in the early 1970s many people who
joined had a New Thought (Religious Science, Unity School of
Christianity) background. They were in mainline Protestant
churches, but they were New Thought in their perspective. As I
traveled the country, I saw that my job offered a great opportunity to do some teaching for some people who otherwise
would not have heard any evangelical speak.

During my years with SFF I developed my concern about
Gnosticism. In terms of its membership, SFF is a Gnostic
organization, pure and simple. Much of its leadership is not. In
terms of the enthusiasm of its local leaders, it appears at times to
be different things in different places—from Spiritualist to fairly orthodox Christian.

ENROTH: I hope you can see why mainstream evangelicals would be deeply troubled by your association with this
group. I don't mean to convey this as a personal criticism of
you. It's just that we find it difficult to understand why someone who identifies himself as an evangelical and who writes for

evangelical periodicals like *Christianity Today* (as well as for *Fate* magazine) would join SFF. How many other mainstream evangelicals are part of the SFF?

MELTON: During the time I was active in SFF (and it has been over seven years since I have even spoken to a group), there were a handful of other evangelicals in SFF. I don't know if that is still the case.

I think the best ministry SFF has—and if it did nothing else, its existence would be justified—consists of its aid to people who have had intense spontaneous psychic experiences. As mentioned above, a large percentage of the population has had such experiences. Some have gone to their pastor only to be told "Oh, that's demonic." The more liberal pastor remarks, "That's a little weird." Worst of all, a pastor has said, "Oh, it's just your imagination." For the person it has been such a strong experience that she or he couldn't deny it. Such people cannot accept either the "demonic" or "weird" hypotheses. Eventually, some of these people find their way to the Spiritual Frontiers Fellowship.

SFF has given me innumerable opportunities to sit down and talk to people about what happened to them. Even to this day some of my fellow pastors send their lay people to me. By word of mouth or through my writings they learn that I know something about the "psychic." People come into my office and describe their out-of-body experience or a deathbed visitation, and then add, "What's wrong with me?" They tell of sitting up in bed in the middle of the night and seeing someone standing there who they know to be dead. It's so vivid, they can't deny it.

Like J. B. Phillips coming home to find C. S. Lewis sitting in his living room, and it's been two years since Lewis died. Lewis speaks to him. Phillips did not record Lewis' words, only mentioned that they were meaningful to him. He said it happened on two occasions, but only on the second occasion did he pay attention. After that, Lewis did not return. People who have experiences like that and who do not have the background and learning of a J. B. Phillips need some place to go to get an explanation of what has happened to them. They need a simple, mundane explanation free of the overtones of either demonism or psychological pathology.

ENROTH: My question as an evangelical is really why you haven't taken advantage of your relationship with the SFF people to more directly and more emphatically—without losing friends or being discourteous—make statements that would be from a more biblical context and that would lead them in more orthodox directions.

Here's an example. In one of your *Spiritual Frontiers* articles you write: "SFF has not called me to be its arbiter of Truth . . . let Truth prosper under whatever label it chooses to manifest." I am not really sure what you had in mind when you wrote that, but my first reaction as a Christian is to say that, SFF aside, you have an obligation as a minister of the gospel to distinguish God's truth from the work of God's adversary, Satan. Not all that proclaims to represent truth is indeed God's Truth.

MELTON: You are quoting from the house organ of SFF. Let's look at the context of the statement. The continual threat to Spiritual Frontiers is that one perspective, particularly one of the more questionable (in Christian terms) perspectives would gain dominance and take over the organization. At the time I wrote the article you are quoting, the threat came from the *Book of Miracles*. It hit SFF like a fad. SFF had just moved its headquarters from Chicago to Independence, Missouri. There was, I perceived, a distinct attempt by many members to align SFF with New Thought. Given the strength of support for the *Book of Miracles* and its close geographic proximity to the Unity School of Christianity, I saw a clear and present danger. The purpose of that article was to say that such an alignment must not occur. If it did, SFF would lose its viability. That was the message to the members at that point.

I realize that as an evangelical I'm in the extreme minority in SFF. The best thing I can do for it is keep it open. If it ever adopted a particular perspective, if it had been taken over by the New Thought people (and today the threat is from the New Age movement), it would mean that the small voice I represent would be cut out entirely. I could no longer present an evangelical perspective.

ENROTH: I would feel badly for you and for evangelicalism if you did not find your faith strengthened within the evangelical community. I would not want to see myself in a position of having to go to such an organization for faith-building purposes. I don't want to be misunderstood—I'm not speaking disrespectfully of them. It's just that they are not mainstream evangelicals and to find a "new dimenion of faith" in such a context rather than with my brothers and sisters in Christ would be most unusual.

MELTON: It's not that I went there and found that new dimension. I want that point to be clearly understood. I happened upon SFF in the late 1960s, and I found there some books that asked some questions I had not been asking. The books sent me to the Bible with new questions. At the same time SFF involved me in a regular discipline of prayer and meditation (that I had dropped from my teen years). I was being forced to ask some questions and look at the Bible in a new light.

Question: You were raised in an evangelical Methodist church in the south, were you not?

MELTON: I was raised on the Scofield Bible by a United Methodist pastor, Alton Parris, who is still the biggest Christian influence on my life. When I went to seminary, I was missing an inner experience that could carry me through. During my last year in seminary and on into graduate school, Alton's teaching was what kept me going. I think I had inherited the best brand of evangelicalism going. He continually preached to us that the three most important things in our Christian life were prayer, Bible study, and witnessing. He said that is what it boils down to, and he lived what he preached. I remember his spending one whole year on Wednesday nights just teaching us to pray, and another year just teaching us to witness, and he covered a good portion of Scripture chapter by chapter.

When I got to seminary, I discovered that the Bible study and witnessing had taken hold, but the prayer hadn't. But he had given me such a thirst for what he seemed to have. I just didn't know how to do it very well, and no one at the seminary communicated it to me. I'm very grateful to SFF for that. It's a small thing in one sense, but it changed my life.

ENROTH: In another article that you wrote entitled, "A Minister Speaks Out on the Psychic and the Devil" . . . .

MELTON: I claim the article but reject the title!

ENROTH: . . . I sense a bitterness toward evangelicalism. You speak disparagingly of Christians attacking the psychic as being of the devil. You speak of "devil theology." You say that Satan is a major figure in "their" literature, especially in the writing of Hal Lindsey who, you write, "seems determined to prove Satan's existence." It sounds to me like you're putting down those of us who take seriously the existence of God's Adversary.

You continue: "One is tempted to dismiss this literature as the ravings of people who know little about their topics . . . . If any central charge can be leveled at the Pentecostal devil-psychic theory, it is shallow biblicism." Those are strong words. Now I am not saying that all evangelicals endorse Hal Lindsey's scholarship or his biblical interpretation. But I certainly would not agree with your characterization of him as being a psychologically dangerous writer.

You say that the central problem of "antipsychic" material is its orientation toward the negative, toward evil and the devil. Evangelical Christians maintain that the Bible—both Old and New Testaments—is very oriented toward the reality of evil and the devil.

You also conclude that the writings of Hal Lindsey and Derek Prince on the demonic are psychologically dangerous literature. "They are major causes of the phenomena they seem most to abhor." I would like you to comment on these statements and explain why you feel so strongly on this topic.

MELTON: Part of it grows out of my research on contemporary Satanism, by which I mean the actual worship of His Infernal Majesty. One fact became quite clear: the material that carries Satanism, from year to year, decade to decade, century to century, is books on Satan and Satanism produced by Chris-

tians. There is no group of Satanists that survives from generation to generation to carry on the tradition. Each generation of
Satanists has been newborn. It basically discovered Satanism by
taking the books of people who wrote about it, i.e., against it,
and decided "Hey, that's a really neat thing, let's do it."

Second, I attended a Pentecostal prayer group for several
years and did quite a bit of running around with Full Gospel
people. Two images stick in my mind so clearly. First is one
popular Pentecostal speaker and his little brown bags. Just the
sheer power that his negative suggestions had on the members
of his audience as they started to regurgitate their lunch.

The other concerns a woman who was having an epileptic
seizure in the hall outside a gathering at which Francis McNutt
was to speak. Her parents had brought her to the meeting
because they wanted to see if she could be healed. Just before
the meeting as people were going into the hall, she had a
seizure. All of a sudden a Pentecostal minister appeared and
started to do an exorcism on her. She was lying on the floor.
She needed someone who knew what he or she was doing to
open her mouth and get her tongue out of her throat, and here
stood this minister shouting, "Devil, come out." He was merely
exacerbating the situation. Finally someone pushed him out of
the way and took care of the situation.

ENROTH: I'm glad you shared that. Your comments
helped me to see your perspective more fully. I had no idea that
you had had personal contact with Derek Prince and other
pentecostalists. I hear what you are saying and agree in part. I
share your concern about some exorcisms and a preoccupation
with Satan. I see a lot of that, too, some of which I believe is
unhealthy. But I didn't know of your past experiences when I
read this article. The background stuff doesn't come through. It
sounds as if you are criticizing all Christians who take Satan
seriously.

MELTON: I see writers such as Lindsey giving the devil
more than he is due. We should give the devil his due, but no
more. That's my real problem: Things that cry out for a mundane explanation get caught up in an imaginary world of

demonism.

Let me share one story few seem to know, at least in the evangelical community; I could never sit in a Katherine Kuhlman meeting without thinking about it. There is Kuhlman doing her thing. And I have read that little-known biography of her by Allen Spraggett. I know what was happening to her. To evangelicals a perfectly acceptable person, but to a knowledgeable observer she's entranced. She told Spraggett what happens to her in a healing service. She began to preach, and all of a sudden she felt herself going out of her body. Something, someone, was taking control, so she quickly ended her sermon and floated out of her body. She watched the healing from the top of the auditorium. When the time of healing ended, whatever took possession of her body left, and she came back into it. I do not think many people are aware of that aspect of her healings.

Thus, I see a real need for some sophistication on the level of the psychic and trying to understand the experiences of people. We need to do it without the mystification of a naive supernaturalism. After you have hung around psychic people and examined psychic claims, it all becomes very mundane. We all have a little bit of ESP. We all have an ability to occasionally sense something we could not have known by more normal means or change things in the world by other than mundane mechanics. Such abilities are like a monkey wrench, neither good nor bad, except as you put them to some use.

ENROTH: Incidentally, I see as one of the characteristics of the growing aberrational Christian groups an incredible preoccupation with the demonic. They've got these deliverance meetings all the time, weekly, sometimes daily. The group in Seattle known as Community Chapel and Bible Training Center is a case in point. I have had people call me just frightened to death as a result of the "deliverance ministry" of this church. One woman told of being dragged physically into meetings and having demons exorcised. She was confused and uncertain: "I'm a Christian. Can this happen to me?" They cast out demons to the point where people are terribly confused, very upset, and psychologically traumatized. I told this same woman, "I think you've been victimized by people who use scare tactics and other kinds of incredible means of control over you—all in the name of Christianity."

It's very popular these days for people to cast out demons —from unbelievers as well as from Christians. Let me add that I *do* believe in the reality of demons and the necessity of spiritual warfare. I don't know of a single cult watcher who doesn't. I also believe in the need for exorcism and that the Lord equips some people to counsel and work in this difficult area. All that I'm saying is that there is a disturbing tendency in these marginal groups to emphasize the power and activity of Satan more than the victorious work of Christ. That's a matter for pause and concern.

4

WHAT IS HERESY?

Question: What precisely is "heresy" and how should Christians relate to it?

MELTON: I would define heresy as being a heterodox form of Christianity, that is, a form of Christianity that deviates from the orthodox tradition on a major point of doctrine. It denies one of the major affirmations of traditional faith. For example, the denial of Jesus' divinity or his humanity would be heresy. The term properly applies only to Christian groups. It does not apply, for example, to the Hare Krishnas, TM, or Witchcraft. One of the problems that led to the great witchhunts of the Middle Ages concerned the relationship of Witchcraft to heresy. Traditionally, the Church had defined Witchcraft as non-Christian. However, in 1484 it redefined it as Satanism, a form of heresy, and therefore brought it under the aegis of the Inquisition, which happened to be sitting idle at that moment (the West being temporarily out of heretics). That redefinition set off the witchhunts (as well as perpetuated the popular notion that Witchcraft and Satanism are the same thing).

Comment: I gather Ron is feeling that you at one point say that Unification theology is a heresy and I know in your more re-

cent article in *Christianity Today* you say it should not be treated
as heresy . . .

MELTON: I say that very clearly in the article that was published in the December 16, 1983, issue. Unification theology is
a totally new religious gestalt that draws upon Christianity
along with several other religions. It's quite a synthesis. That's
the view I've pretty well always held.

Comment: Let's discuss the question of reincarnation.

MELTON: I've written continually about reincarnation. I am
very much opposed to it. I got involved in the question because
of the Edgar Cayce reincarnation book that Noel Langley wrote.
That volume was a historical atrocity, and I wrote an article for
Fate refuting it. That was the start. Since then I have spoken many
times on the subject, written several articles, and that *Fate* article
has been reprinted I don't know how many times.

It got to be quite an item in Spiritual Frontiers Fellowship,
since I had become the major person who would speak openly
and broadly against reincarnation. I remember one of my
friends joking with me after one session. She opened up in front
of everyone and said, "Gordon, I don't think you even believed
in reincarnation the last two or three times you were here."

I was book editor for *Fate* for five years, and I can
remember one Hindu writer who had written several books on
reincarnation who refused to send us any of his books for
review. As he put it, "Reincarnation books never get a fair
review in *Fate.*"

I have been thinking of doing a full-size book on the topic;
I even have my notes together and my outline done. Mean-
while there are several good Christian critiques on the market.

ENROTH: What do you think about InterVarsity's new
book on it—the one by Mark Albrecht?

MELTON: I share his views almost totally. I do wish Albrecht was somewhat more sophisticated and knowledgeable
about parapsychology. His critique of Ian Stevenson is weak,

and the entire book could have been strengthened if he had been familiar with the literature in psychical research. But in the main, I agree with his approach.

ENROTH: I'm not playing the devil's advocate, but as long as we're on this—we're confused when we read statements like the following from your *Fate* magazine article on the topic of interest in reincarnation. You say, "It must be looked at especially by Christians with the full knowledge that the total witness of Jesus, the Bible, and Christian spokesmen of the past will give no support. However, the cause is not lost on this account, merely hindered. While Scripture and early church writings have a certain normative value for the Christian faith, as well as high standing for their general philosophical and religious value, they are only a few of the many expressions of the church's life and thought." That raises some eyebrows. Would you comment on these statements?

MELTON: That's an example on my softening a critique for an audience of total believers in reincarnation. I pulled my punch, but in spite of my holding back, that article provoked more mail, almost all hostile, than any article *Fate* published in the year before or after.

As a historian, I was also drawing on an analogy. The specific example was evolution. Until one gets to the nineteenth century, there is no support for evolution from the history of the church or the Bible. There is a strong witness against evolution, at least in some forms, in Scripture. In spite of that, there is pretty widespread acceptance of evolution today, even among evangelicals. At that point I was drawing the analogy that reincarnation could possibly find the same kind of acceptance some day.

ENROTH: Do you think that will happen with reincarnation?

MELTON: Hard to say. I hope it doesn't. Reincarnation is a tremendously popular idea. It is held by many of our church members who keep silent about their beliefs. Twenty-three percent of the American public believe it. That's a force of opinion to contend with. The article you cited was published in the

Spiritual Frontiers *Journal*. Subsequent to its publication, the Institute for the Study of American Religion, which I head, did a survey and found that eighty-eight percent of the SFF members were reincarnationists. I had no idea it was so high. It really shook me, but then it explained the reaction I was getting to my talks on the subject. Whenever I spoke, the hostility from the audience would run quite high.

Let me add that I wrote that particular article in direct response to Noel Langley's book and others I found in tracking down his sources. There is a tradition of writings that, beginning in theosophy in the late nineteenth century and continuing through the New Thought movement and the work of Edgar Cayce, talks about a fifth-century conspiracy to edit reincarnation out of the Bible. The real hammer I deliver is in sayng to them, if you want to believe in reincarnation you must do so in the full knowledge that Jesus, the apostolic church and the patristic fathers all disapproved of the idea. You will have to find another basis. There was no conspiracy.

ENROTH: Yes, I saw that in the article. I guess our main concern would be why you don't make a stronger statement than that Scripture and early church writings have only a certain normative value. Evangelicals would say Scripture has a very definite defining normative value.

MELTON: I would entirely agree with you at that point. For me, Scripture and the early church have normative value. Wesley's hermeneutics were very well stated at that point. First, we look to Scripture. Second, if there is a point of interpretation in dispute, we look to the church fathers of the first few centuries. If the point remains unresolved, we use the best reason and tradition (à la Luther) that we can.

But remember that the article was directed to an audience of largely liberal Protestants, many of whom do not share our view of Scripture, and an even larger audience who do not accept Scripture at all (unless it happens to accord with what they otherwise believe).

ENROTH: My own definition of heresy—again I'm not a theologian—but I would agree with James Sire. He speaks of "doctrines and/or practices that contradict those of the Scriptures as interpreted by traditional Christianity as represented by the major Catholic and Protestant denominations and as expressed in such statements as the Apostles' Creed." That's how I view heresy.

MELTON: Now I would be much more specific than that, and I would say doctrines and opinions held by people who call themselves Christians. What I'm saying is that Hindus and Buddhists should not be called heretics.

ENROTH: Yes, by that definition they wouldn't be. I don't feel that in the sense that Sire uses it Buddhists or Hindus could be called Christian heretics.

Question: In other words, you say they're nonevangelical or nonorthodox and that's not enough. You've also got to say that they share a basically biblical framework. Otherwise they go beyond being a heresy and end up being another religion. Why did you feel that was an important question?

ENROTH: Maybe it's because of my imagery of frequently referring to these other groups as false religions. Alternative religions, fine. As an academician I have no problems with that. But as a Christian, I would say, rather than heretical religions, false religions.

MELTON: However, in your lead essay in the InterVarsity publication *A Guide to Cults and New Religions* you use the term "heresy" to include all the cults. Half the groups discussed in the book are clearly not Christian, and therefore not heretical groups. You need to make that distinction in talking about alternative religions.

Comment: Gordon, would you state why you felt non-Christian religions needed to be brought up in the light of heresy and in the light of Ron's lead essay?

MELTON: I think we have to make a place in our thinking, again on a practical level, for non-Christian religions in this country. Their presence is growing and becoming an important part of the social and political fabric. We need to take them more seriously and realistically than we have in the past. They are no longer small groups on the edge of culture that can be dismissed. They have entered in force and now command positions of influence and respect.

Eastern religions test our ability to cope. If we see them as just the minor products of a few eccentric and power hungry gurus, we misjudge what is happening. These Eastern cults are the missionary army of the East, and all trends suggest that just as Christianity was carried around the world in the last century, so Hinduism and Buddhism will be in this century. The United States will soon be a microcosm of the world religious situation.

As Christians we have to stop playing games in terms of our understanding of what is occurring. We have to take Eastern religion as seriously as we evangelicals have begun to take Judaism. We have to be able to judge the various Eastern faiths, both in their particularity and as the representatives of other great world faiths. We must find some way of relating to them, both dialogically and missionally.

I don't have any great insights or answers at this point, but I wonder, Ron, how you see non-Christian religions? Do you see some as closer, more positive than others . . . Judaism closer than Buddhism? I must emphasize that I take Paul, for example, very seriously when he says that what is not of faith is sin.

ENROTH: I also take Paul very seriously when he says that which is not of faith is sin. I see non-Christian religions as being outside the faith.

MELTON: The implication for me is that Hinduism and other religions, each in its own different way, are preparing people to become Christians. In one sense, if you are outside of the church, it does not matter. Each of the major faith traditions are on an equal footing. I do not give Judaism one up on Islam or Buddhism or Hinduism. I see each as schoolmasters that can lead to Christ, so to speak. That also affects my opinion of them. I would not denegrate Judaism, but I would view it with the same eyes with which I view Eastern groups. I would judge

Judaism with the same standards as I judge Buddhism. I see a person in an Eastern religion as having just as much preparation to receive the gospel as I would a person raised a Jew.

The bottom line is that we should treat Buddhism and Hinduism with the same respect we give Judaism.

ENROTH: That would be interesting to explore with some comparative religion scholars. In other words, you don't really see a difference between Judaism and its view of God and Eastern groups such as Hinduism and their view of deities. You would handle them the same. The God of the Old Testament and the deities of Hinduism are not really different?

MELTON: On that one issue, Hinduism and Judaism certainly vary. I see Judaism as preparing people to receive the gospel through the idea of the one God and the Law, whereas I see Eastern religions as preparing people to receive the gospel through the ideas of spirituality and the experience of transcendence. When we get into Hasidism and Sufism, the mystical forms of Judaism and Islam, the distinctions become somewhat blurred. Hasidic Judaism is the major source of our occultism in the West. The Sufis are now challenging orthodox (Sunni) Islam for an audience in the West.

That's the intent of my remarks. All the great religions prepare people, and if we use the same criteria to judge each, it might just soften our harsh rhetoric toward things Eastern.

Question: You're saying, Gordon, that when Paul said the law is a schoolmaster to bring us to Christ, he's speaking basically to a Jewish audience, and if he were speaking today to our pluralistic culture in America he would say all religions are schoolmasters to bring us to Christ. Do the Old Testament prophets say that alternative religions are ways people can come to God?

MELTON: No, that's not what I am saying. I am saying that all the great religious traditions are preparing people to receive Christ. Some individual religions are doing nothing of the sort. Some individual groups are corrupt, are hotbeds of moral bankruptcy, are leading people into negative lives. They are the exception and can be found in all the religious traditions. We had ours in the form of Jim Jones.

The Old Testament prophets were, I think, speaking out against such religions—the sacrifice of children, superstitions, etc. At the same time we must recognize the growth within the Old Testament as God spoke to the Hebrew children. We no longer approve of law codes that condone the wasting of conquered cities or the execution of juvenile delinquents. In like measure, I am not sure that the prophets would have stood up and said, "Let's all become Christians." The first century Jews didn't exactly rush into the church.

Question: There is a strong emphasis upon the Lord, the one true God, and the fact that one day all will worship Him in Jerusalem and worship Him as the only true God. Would they say that these other gods that were being worshiped were preparing people religiously to worship the Lord? How about Paul or the New Testament apostles? Would they feel as you do that the gods in Greece and elsewhere were like the law?

MELTON: There's certainly one example of it. As Paul stood on Mars Hill in Athens, he said, "The one you worship ignorantly, I come to proclaim." He had found the "unknown God" a preparation for his message.

At the same time Paul became sucked into a very practical problem, the conflict caused by meat that had been sacrificed to idols being brought into the Christian communal meals.

ENROTH: How about Scientology in that regard?

MELTON: Scientology is an odd case about which I have not reached a final judgment. I have a much better opinion of them since Heber Jentsch took over the top office and they have cleaned house to a certain extent. The Guardian's Office was corrupt from the word go, and Scientology still has some distance to go to rid itself of the effects of actions generated by that office. It had been set up to be a sort of "defenders of the faith" structure. The original idea was that the Guardian's Office would handle the attacks upon the church so that the great body of members would not have to worry about them . . . they could go on with their classes and auditing.

It was the hard core of the Guardian's Office who were caught and convicted several years ago for the break-ins and thefts in Washington, D.C. They were the source of the dirty tricks and the enemies' files. Almost everything you can say nasty about Scientology that is true originated in the Guardian's Office.

Question: Did they do this with or without Ron Hubbard's blessing?

MELTON: That we do not know. In his last tape to the church he condemned those who had been caught for departing from Scientology directives and trying to live above them. On the other hand, very little that was important went on in the church without his knowledge. He, of course, has not been a member of the church for many years. I just don't know.

In any case, the break with the past, the cleanup, began when the church decided not to support the appeal of those convicted in Washington. It withdrew financial support for any appeal. I would not say it is totally reformed (the corruption went too deep), but I would say that at least one person at the top and his staff are trying to clean things up, though they are having to constantly fight off the brush fires caused by the remnants of the old Guardian's Office tricks. I remember the new head of the church, Heber Jentsch, telling me some months ago, "Gordon, when I took over this office, it was like every day I came in and there was a new paper on my desk. I would read through it and say to myself, 'We did what?'" I will say in all honesty that I will be sorely disappointed if I discover in the future that Jentsch was and is a part of any Scientology corruption.

I think the story of the Church of Scientology is one of the most complicated and intriguing stories of twentieth-century religion. I have told several people that one of my ambitions for

my retirement years is to write a history of Scientology. I'm
hoping that the controversy will have died down and that I can
get into the archives and find out what really happened.

For the present I will withhold final judgment on Scientology. There has certainly been corruption, and at least some
Scientology leaders have been guilty of a portion of the nasty
things that people have claimed they have. At the same time,
just as undeniably, they have had equally evil things done to
them and some anti-Scientologists are no less corrupt than the
worst in Scientology.

I told Artie Mauren, a former public relations person for
the church, what I thought their basic flaw was: "Artie, you've
got an ethic that says, 'Don't get mad, get even,' and that ethic is
going to do you in." Their eye-for-an-eye approach led them to
retaliate on minor matters and make enemies out of mild critics.
The Guardian's Office declared war, and the government and
many individuals joined the battle.

ENROTH: You're probably the only evangelical who's on
good terms with such Scientology leaders as Jentsch and
Mauren. How do you explain it? Don't they ever get offended
at you? Because you present biblical truth?

MELTON: Certainly they do. I thought a time or two
while I was doing the *Encyclopedia of American Religions* we
would come to blows. But it has always been the Church of
Scientology's stated position—and I have held them to it—that
you can print anything at all about them as long as it's true. It is
all right to say the church is unbiblical and un-Christian, but just
don't repeat lies. That was their whole approach with me. As
with other controversial groups, I submitted what I wrote about
them to the church and even sent a copy to Ron Hubbard
before publishing it, and I asked their comment upon it. If you
had read all I have written, you would have seen some pretty
nasty things about them, and they have not liked what I wrote
at times. But they did not have a problem with either me or my
evangelical Christianity. Their problem has always been with
people who they felt printed lies about them. That is a constant
theme in their litigation.

ENROTH: Yes, they've also asked me to give my material to them before it is published. They've said, "We'll make your paper more scholarly." My experience with them has been, contrary to what you said, that anything negative said about them, including my own negative evaluation of them, ends up being interpreted by them as "antireligious." Their critics are labeled "antireligious." Because I evaluate Scientology (or any other group) in the context of biblical Christianity in a way they don't like, I am somehow antireligious. Scientologists and other APRL members have on occasion demonstrated outside of the sites where I am scheduled to speak. They carry placards announcing that anticultists are opposed to freedom of religion. That is so ridiculous and untrue, but that's their response to what they perceive as negative evaluation of them and/or other new religious movements. I think it's a sad commentary on the time in which we live when we've reached the point where we don't in some contexts have the freedom to evaluate other groups in terms of our own particular perspective and faith lest we get threatened with a lawsuit, or become targets of harassment.

That's not only the case with regard to Scientology. I think one of the most serious problems facing evangelical authors today is the harassment that we receive not only from representatives of non-Christian religions, but from our own brothers and sisters in Christ who are so upset by a negative evaluation of them that they threaten legal action. Christian publishers will say, "We'll publish your material, Enroth, but don't mention groups X, Y, and Z." How is the Christian public going to be informed about questionable religious groups if authors are muzzled by legal intimidation? It's a matter of freedom of speech, as I see it.

Comment: On the other side, evangelical publishers will threaten you with a lawsuit if you criticize what they've published.

MELTON: I think one of the problems we face in writing

about other groups is accuracy. We evangelicals often do not accurately portray the beliefs and thought world of the groups we write about. The inaccuracies that fill some popular Christian books on cults, (and here I think of Bob Larson's *Book of Cults* and *Understanding the Cults* by Josh McDowell and Don Stewart) derive from an initial hostility that informs their research of a cult group. "It's only a cult, so I don't have to really treat it with the same care that, for example, I would a book by a theologian I respected," they seem to say. That hostility is combined with a lack of desire to really understand the inner dynamics of the group. We gather just enough information to refute it, to score debating points against it. That attitude leads to shallow, mistake-filled writing.

I write from a different perspective. My first concern is not to refute or say anything derogatory. I assume that the members and leaders of a group are honest people, people of religious integrity, who have come to their faith out of honest aspirations and motives. I assume that the Spirit of God has been working with them leading them to the point to which they have come. In learning about them I am trying to enter their world and truly comprehend what is happening to them. As a Christian I ask what preparation God has made for these people to hear and respond to the gospel.

Thus while on a practical level I know that Hinduism is likely to grow and become a religious force in the United States, on a personal and theological level I meet a Hindu (or a Buddhist or a Scientologist) as a not-yet Christian. Rather than point the condemnatory finger at the non-Christian or anti-Christian, I want to present the hand of friendship and love to the potential Christian.

Thus I try to make the distinctions between evangelical Christianity and other faiths, but I try to do so matter-of-factly. I try to do so without throwing out derogatory labels at people with whom I disagree.

This warning I would apply to the use of the term cult. When you call someone, some group, a cultist or a cult today, it's like calling that person or movement Communist. You are not just saying the people are wrong, that they differ from evangelical Christianity. You are saying that they are loathsome creatures, slime monsters, something to be despised and rejected. If you go around calling your neighbor a Communist, you open yourself up to a libel suit. That's public defamation of character. We have reached the situation that calling a group a cult is almost the same thing.

ENROTH: I'm hearing what you're saying about labels. When you use the label "cult" these days, it's necessary that you be careful and sensitive. I know I try to be sensitive about this sort of thing, but the new religious groups don't always see it that way. More mutual respect is needed.

5

HOW SHOULD CHRISTIANS RELATE TO CULT MEMBERS?

Question: What is the best way for Christians to relate to cult members?

ENROTH: I think first of all we need to have more awareness of these groups—whatever label we use to define them. There needs to be increased information before we can make statements, evaluative or otherwise, about them. We have to have objective, accurate information. I think in the evangelical community it would be wise for every large church to have a "cult watcher" in its midst—someone who's interested in new religious movements and whose task it is to keep up on all of the information available concerning these groups—in the form of books, films, and tapes, someone who can be in touch with organizations like the Spiritual Counterfeits Project and similar organizations to read all the stuff that's coming out.

In that sense we need an educational ministry, starting at the junior high school level. We need to begin to help young people theologize. I'm not sure how that's to be done, but I think we need to recognize that some of our approach to Christian education, including information about new/alternative religions, has been rather shallow, if not absent. There's been a

vacuum in our curriculum and in our teaching with regard to
this area. We need to help people, young people especially, to
ask the right questions—to develop what I call "discernment
skills."

Second, I think we need to present an alternative model to
cults and new religions—an alternative model of commitment
and spiritual reality, that as we have an opportunity to witness
to individuals involved in cults and new religions, they will see
in us a positive, vital, and even dramatic faith. And I don't mean
by that merely substituting one subjective experience for
another, and getting caught in the trap of saying, "My experience is better than yours." The gospel is not based on
testimonials.

We need to help them to see God's truth as it is revealed in
his Word, and the relationship of that truth to our everyday
lives, and the necessity and possibility of having a personal
relationship with Jesus Christ. It's been my experience that,
rather than spending a great deal of time arguing with people or
even engaging in discussions of a strictly biblical nature, we
need to impress upon people the reality of a personal encounter
with the God of the Bible. That really gets through.

Cultists often think that only their group is serious about
spiritual things. They need to see in us something vital and real
and life-transforming. Unfortunately, for many Christians that
testimony may not be there, and that then becomes an indict-
ment of the churches and of us as individual Christians.

Once cultists see the alternative model combined with a
loving witness, hopefully they'll be more open to what we have
to say. I agree with "Jerry" Yamamoto, author of *The Puppet
Master*, who said that a personal witness has to be sincere,
respectful, loving, and very warm. We should not begin by putting down their leaders. At some point, of course, we need to
examine their teaching. But that's not the way to begin the
dialogue.

So I differ from some of the traditional cult watchers and
cult critics who come on very strong in condemning the leaders
of some of these groups. An aggressive, confrontational ap-

proach is not, in my opinion, the way to go. I think we need to be patient, and we need to be prepared for a continuing dialogue. It is not something that will happen overnight. Our attitude is so important. We must accept cult members as persons and affirm their basic search. Then they'll be more open to what we have to say.

MELTON: Amen. I'm in complete agreement with everything Ron has just said.

I would merely add a few things that we as people interested in a ministry to cult members need to do. First, we need a change of focus. We've put a lot of time and energy into a very few groups, and very little into those that have been the most successful in terms of recruiting new members. If you try to find a Christian evaluation of Swami Muktananda and his followers, it's very hard to locate. Yet here is a group with approximately one hundred and forty centers in the United States, and several times the members the Unification Church can claim. Moon in twenty years of evangelism in America has netted only six to seven thousand members and there are only twenty-five hundred active Hare Krishna initiates. Think how much ink has been spilled on those two groups to the neglect of the more successful ones.

Question: Could you name some of the more neglected but successful groups?

MELTON: Tibetan Buddhism is growing by leaps and bounds. During the last five years over fifty centers have appeared in all parts of the United States.

Others among the most neglected would be the Sufi Order headed by Pir Vilayat Khan; the Johannine Daist Communion, also known as the Dawn Horse Communion or the Free Primitive Church of Divine Communion, headed by Da Free John (also known as Franklin Jones and Bubba Free John); the Ruhani Satsang headed by Kirpal Singh's several successors (it divided into three groups after Singh's death); and ECKANKAR. It is a shame that the most substantive Christian response to Baha'i thought is the chapter in Ron's last book.

Second, in our criticism of groups, we need to be a bit more sophisticated about money. Most people seem to be very unaware of how much money it takes to run any kind of religious organization, especially one that is national in scope. Most are unaware of the cost of property in urban centers or the value of office buildings owned by even small evangelical groups. If we are going to complain about what we think might be an outlandish budget by a group of which we disapprove, then we have to adopt the same standards for judging our churches and synagogues. Religion is big business, no matter who does it. Any group trying to grow, expand geographically, and institutionalize must have a large cash flow. And it doesn't take a lot of people pooling their financial resources to create a big budget.

Thus when we assess the money, the cash flow, of so-called cults, we must do so in light of the cash flow of similar, more acceptable groups. Are Moon's cash flow, capital assets, and financial resources out of line when compared to, just for example, the Billy Graham Evangelistic Association, or more closely, the Oral Roberts Ministries? The media talked of the Unification Church's purchases of hundreds of thousands of dollars of property. In fact, the church bought a set of thirty-year mortgages. Unlike some older churches with millions sitting in endowments, the Unification Church is continually thirty days from bankruptcy. As a matter of fact, it almost went under in the months following the giant wedding in New York.

ENROTH: Scientology, too, is very weak financially.

MELTON: Those groups that have been in court have suffered greatly. The Krishnas are threatened with the loss of all their California assets because of the George case. We don't stop to think about that.

Similarly, when we view a non-Christian group we have to understand that it will use money differently from Christians. For example, in the light of Krishna theology, the Krishnas are following a logical pattern in building the expensive buildings in West Virginia. Outside of Wheeling they are creating a

Western version of the Hindu holy city of Vrindvan. They have built a palatial mansion that was to be the home of Swami Bhaktivedanta. It's now a shrine. They are also building an ornate temple. If we attack them for putting so much money into those buildings, we must attack the theology that allows it. At the same time we must consider Christian building enterprises —the Cathedral of St. John the Divine, Oral Roberts University, the glass cathedral of Robert Schuler, etc.

I raise the issue of *money* because when it comes to cults I think it is *a false issue.* Top religious leaders of all stripes are much more motivated by power than money. While some leaders from Rajneesh to Roberts try to demonstrate an opulent life style as a means of demonstrating the truth of their teachings, even that opulence fades beside the power they exercise over followers. Bhaktivedanta, the guru of the Krishnas, by all reports lived an austere life of material renunciation but was revered as divine. He wielded tremendous power. Even while we see the large amount of money that Moon controls for the Unification Church, many of the earlier followers report that they found the church attractive because of seeing the rather simple lifestyle lived by Moon on a personal level.

ENROTH: Two additional observations on our relating to cult members. We have to be careful to temper that relationship (and the tolerance I think we need to have) with the realization that it could lead to a compromising of our position. I say it could. It need not and should not, but it could lead to a compromise because it's easy for us to become so tolerant that we fail to discern and distinguish that which, from a biblical position, clearly constitutes error. I think we need to share our Christian convictions in love and identify those distinctions that we hold dear. But loving people does not save them. They must come to see their sin and then appropriate the grace of Christ Jesus.

Second, I think a totally neglected area in the church these days is the tremendous need for resources, counseling, and resocialization support for people who have come out of cults and aberrational Christian groups.

For example, I know of two young adults who recently left a self-improvement cult in which they had held leadership for several years. While members, they lived a very austere lifestyle. They didn't get much money as workers in this organization, and yet they've given so many years of their life to this group. It's as if they're going through a bereavement. They don't have a job, they have no money. Good friends have been left behind. They're confused and anxious at this point.

They're very typical of people I know who are coming out of these groups. Another example: the Love Family, also known as the Church of Armageddon, in Seattle is now falling apart. Their guru, Love Israel, has been discovered to have feet of clay by his followers. The cult has started to disintegrate. There are several hundred people involved, some of whom have been members for years. It's the only life that they know. Who is going to be around to pick up the pieces? This is especially urgent when the cult involved is a totalistic milieu fostering extreme dependency. It's open to question as to how well they will be able to function outside.

I am confronted on a weekly basis with a truly desperate need for an alternative to some of the approaches of well-intentioned deprogrammers who, nevertheless, are unconcerned about spiritual needs. As Christians we should not exploit people coming out of the cults and immediately try to zap them with an invitation to get involved with the First Baptist Church, or whatever. I think they're very vulnerable emotionally, and we have to handle them with care, and respect the fact that they're going through a very difficult time. As we have opportunity, we need to gently introduce them to Jesus Christ —whose yoke *is* easy, as Scripture reminds us. Many people exiting from cults are burned out on religion and find it difficult to trust religious authority figures again.

The point is that I am confronted on a regular basis with hurting people who are coming out of these groups, and there are no halfway houses or rehabilitation centers that I can refer them to. The evangelical church and the church at large have done a great deal for other types of social needs. They've provided resources for unwed mothers, for drug addicts, and for alcoholics. But they have done nothing for the person who is coming out of one of these extremist cults. Christians are not aware of the great need to assist former cultists on the path back into mainstream society.

I feel very strongly about this need. It involves a ministry of reconciliation, healing, and nurturing. It is a real need that has to be addressed, and it's going unmet. I know of nowhere in the United States where I can refer people, even if they had the money, to a program staffed with sincere, concerned, sensitive counselors who are aware of the dynamics of the cultic lifestyle and who can understand the reentry process. Many pastors and others want to help and are sincere, but they don't really know where these people are coming from. Former cultists have special needs and special problems. One is that they often find misunderstanding and even stigma in the evangelical community. I challenge Christians to extend fellowship and friendship to this new minority—the former cultists.

One final observation. The primary calling of the church is to proclaim the gospel. The church's main objective should not be to combat the cults. That does not mean that we do not have an obligation to be informed, sensitive, concerned Christians when it comes to the topic of cults. Awareness of the cult problem is terribly important. But primacy must always be given to the task of bearing witness to the gospel of Jesus Christ. It's easy for some Christians to get caught up in a "single issue" crusader mentality vis-à-vis the cults, and I don't think that's what we're called to do.

MELTON: It is heartening, having been brought together to air our differences on cult-related issues, that we have discovered so high a level of agreement, especially here in these summary remarks. I am encouraged that as we came to the close of this rather lengthy session and hurried to say the important things about what we should do and where we should go, a basic consensus emerged. To discover that mutual ground as a basis for future research, speaking, and writing has made the time expended more than worthwhile.

6

A BASIC REFERENCE SHELF ON CULTS

It is our belief that every local congregation should have at least one person who is familiar with cults and can supply accurate information to the membership about them. The preceding discussion pointed out the often bewildering array of alternative religious groups, particularly the newer and more nonconventional ones which are challenging the contemporary church. Truthful and factual information about these groups can both allay unnecessary fears when encountering them and provide helpful assistance in making a Christian witness in any confrontation. The following publications are recommended for inclusion in a church's library as helpful resources. This list begins with general reference books which survey the field of cult activities. From the large number of Christian books generally available we have selected those we believe to be among the best of those we have seen. A few volumes which deal with a specific prominent group have also been included. And for the more serious reader, we have selected a list of the best scholarly studies.

Surveying the Field

Only one work has attempted to cover all the religious

groups currently active in the United States. *The Encyclopedia of American Religions* (1978) by J. Gordon Melton covers more than 1,300 churches and other less-conventional religious groups, including all of those groups we have generally termed cults. This encyclopedia gives basic information on each group's history, beliefs, and organization. The three volumes, though expensive, are a must for gaining an overall picture of America's growing religious pluralism. The set can be ordered from Gale Research Co., Book Tower, Detroit, MI 48225. Also helpful, and supplemental to the list of books recommended here, are the *Index to Countercult Resources* (Acts 17, Box 2183, La Mesa, CA 92041) and *An Annotated Bibliography of Literature Related to New Religious Movements* (Spiritual Counterfeits Project, Box 4308, Berkeley, CA 94704).

The major new religions are surveyed in depth in *A Guide to Cults & New Religions* by Ronald Enroth and others (Downers Grove, IL: InterVarsity Press, 1983). This volume, which includes treatment of both older groups such as the Latter-day Saints (Mormons), and newer groups such as ECKANKAR and EST, is among the best surveys from a Christian viewpoint on cults produced to date. Also useful is an older volume by Robert S. Ellwood, *Religious and Spiritual Groups in America* (Englewood Cliffs, NJ: Prentice-Hall, 1973). Ellwood, an outstanding history of religions scholar, has produced a volume which covers in some depth groups which elsewhere have received only scant treatment.

The Christian Response to the Cults
As the number of different religions in American has grown, over a hundred specialized ministries to nonconventional religions have emerged. The amount of literature, primarily tracts and pamphlets, these ministries produce is enormous. From the books which have been published to inform the church about cults and the issues which their presence generates, we have selected those titles which we consider to be the best. There are undoubtedly good books not listed below, and their noninclusion should cast no aspersions upon them. It

simply means we were not familiar with them or thought the items we picked were better.

One category of cult books deals with the issues which the presence of cults and a pluralistic religious environment presents to the Christian community. Outstanding among these is Harold Bussell's *Unholy Devotion* (Grand Rapids, MI: Zonder-van, 1983). Bussell argues that the attraction of cults comes not from their doctrines but from their style, the spirituality they offer, coupled with some significant problems in contemporary church life. Ronald Enroth's *The Lure of the Cults* (Downers Grove, IL: InterVarsity Press, (rev. ed.) 1985) follows Bussell's discussion with a more detailed analysis of the attractions of cult life and practical actions which churches and parents of youth can do to guard against that appeal. J. Gordon Melton and Robert L. Moore's *The Cult Experience* (New York: Pilgrim Press, 1982) covers a broad range of topics from the history of alternative religions in America to the deprogramming debate and concludes with a set of guidelines for pastors, churches, counselors, and families who must face the issue of a church member, client, or family member's involvement in a different religion. On the more theological side, James Sire's *Scripture Twisting* (Downers Grove, IL: InterVarsity Press, 1980) covers the most popular ways which individual cult members and groups interpret and in some cases distort scripture. A balanced approach which was produced by the Southern Baptist Office of Interfaith Witness is *Your God, My God* by Mike Creswell and Paul Obregon (Atlanta, GA: Home Missions Board, SBC, 1980).

A fine resource from a Roman Catholic perspective for church families where a son or daughter has joined a cult is John Saliba's little pamphlet, *Religious Cults Today, A Challenge to Christian Families.* It may be ordered from Liquori Publications, One Liguori Drive, Liguori, MO 63057. Finally, though we can not endorse some of the views expressed in Lowell D. Streiker's *Mind Bending* (Garden City, NY: Doubleday, 1984), this volume by the longtime leader of the Freedom Counseling Center is worth reading. He has developed valuable insights from his lengthy interaction with various phases of the cult scene, including members, ex-members, parents, and anticult groups. Streiker's words on deprogramming are particularly valuable.

We would also caution church members about some quite popular books on cult questions, which we cannot fully approve. These include such books as *Snapping* (1978) by Flo Conway and Jim Siegelman; *Let Our Children Go!* (1976) by Ted Patrick, with Tom Dulack; and *Cults in America, Programmed for Paradise* (1983) by Willa Appel. *Snapping*, in particular, carries a lengthy attack upon evangelical Christians and suggests that any form of conversion is illegitimate and amounts to brainwashing. In a similar vein, Patrick suggests that one can become brainwashed simply by reading the Bible, quite apart from membership in any group. Each of these volumes is more or less against any evangelical witness, and each not only condones but advocates coercive deprogramming as a solution to the cult problem.

Outstanding among the introductory material on non-conventional religion is the "Response Series," a set of thirty-two page pamphlets prepared by the Lutheran Church-Missouri Synod and published by Concordia Publishing House. Each one of the eight pamphlets issued to date succinctly informs the reader "How to Respond to . . . " the Cults, Transcendental Meditation, the Lodge, the Latter-day Saints (Mormons), the Occult, Jehovah's Witnesses, Eastern Religions and the New Christian religions. Equally worthy are two titles in a set of pamphlets by Gordon R. Lewis, one on "Confronting Religions of the East," and a second which dicusses Paul's sermon on Mars Hill and its relation to evangelism among non-Christians. They were published in the Seminary Study Series of the Conservative Baptist Theological Seminary (Box 10,000, Denver, CO 80210). Though Lewis's pamphlets are available without charge, when ordering we suggest a small donation to cover printing and mailing costs.

Christian bookstores typically carry a number of books which offer brief chapters on different new religions. Of the ones we have seen, the best and most up-to-date are: *Cults of North America* by Earl Schipper (Grand Rapids, MI: Baker Book House, 1982) which covers Jehovah's' Witnesses, the Latter-day Saints (Mormons), Christian Science, The Unification Church and The Way International. *Today's Sects* by Maurice C. Burrell and J. Stafford Wright (Grand Rapids, MI: Baker Book House, 1983) deals with some of the more established groups: Latter-day Saints (Mormons), Jehovah's Witnesses, the Christadelphians, Christian Science, Spiritualism and Theosophy. Maurice Burrell's *The Challenge of the Cults* (Grand Rapids, MI: Baker Book House, 1982) treats the more noteworthy of the newer groups: Worldwide Church of God, Children of God/Family of Love, the Unification Church, the Divine Light Mission, Transcendental Meditation, the Hare Krishnas, and the Church of Scientology. Finally, William J. Peterson's very fine but now dated *These Curious New Cults* (New Canaan, CT: Keats Publishing Co., 1973) has been revised and updated by the publisher as *Those Curious New Cults in the Eighties* (1982). It comes with a study guide which makes it easily adaptable for use by church school classes.

Some of the older books on cults are still useful and retain an honored place in any church library. They include: Jan Karel Van Baalen, *The Chaos of Cults* (Grand Rapids, MI: Eerdmans, 4th ed. rev., 1962); Russell P. Spittler, *Cults and Isms* (Grand Rapids, MI: Baker Book House, 1962); Gordon R. Lewis, *Confronting the Cults* (Grand Rapids, MI: Baker Book House, 1966); and Edmond C. Gruss, *Cults and the Occult in the Age of Aquarius* (Nutley, NJ: Presbyterian and Reformed Publishing Company, 1974).

The Moonies and Other New Groups

For those interested in an indepth study of one particular group, materials are more difficult to obtain. Some of the largest groups have yet to be given any substantive treatment from a Christian faith perspective, while some relatively small groups (for example the Hare Krishnas) have been given attention far out of proportion to their numbers.

Surely the most famous and controversial of the new religions is the Unification Church (Moonies). Also, few groups have so changed, even on substantive doctrinal matters as have the Moonies, since they first arrived in the United States in 1959. Two of the first books on the Unification Church, *The Puppet Masters* by J. Isamu Yamamoto (1977), and *The Moon Is Not the Son* by James Bjornstad (1976), have become quite dated. Fortunately, both are being revised by Bethany Fellowship: *The Puppet Masters* (Minneapolis, 1985) and, Bjornstad's work under a new title, *Sun Myung Moon and the Unification Church* (Minneapolis, 1984). Among the better Christian reflections on this group are the two books by Chris Elkins, *Heavenly Deception* (Wheaton, IL: Tyndale House Publishers, 1980) and *What Do You Say to a Moonie?* (Wheaton, IL: Tyndale House Publishers, 1981). Eileen Barker's *The Making of a Moonie, Brainwashing or Choice?* (Oxford: Basil Blackwell, 1984) is a fine survey by an outstanding sociologist, and is based on several years of research. Following the lead of Elkins' books, it does much to break many of the common, but false, stereotypes of cult life.

Among the numerous books on the Unification Church, evangelical Christians may find especially interesting one published by the Unification Church itself, the *Evangelical-Unification Dialogue* (1979), edited by Richard Quebedeaux and Rodney Sawatsky. In 1978, at the height of the tension created by the Unification Church, a group of evangelical scholars including Roy Carlisle, Joseph Hopkins, Patrick Means, and John and Letha Scanzoni traveled to Barrytown, New York, for two discussion sessions. Numerous issues and objections to the Unification Church were aired, to which members of the Church gave their response. This 374-page paperback volume may be ordered from Rose of Sharon Press, P.O. Box 2432, New York, NY 10116.

The Children of God, recently renamed the Family of Love, have received treatment in two excellent books. Deborah Davis, daughter of Children of God founder David Berg, left the group several years ago and has written a moving and detailed account of life inside the group, *The Children of God* (Grand Rapids, MI: Zondervan, 1984). It should be read along side of *The Snare of the Fowler* by Frankie Fonde Brodie (Grand Rapids, MI: Zondervan, 1982), the story of a mother's spiritual pilgrimage after her son joined the Children of God.

Other noteworthy books which treat a single group include: Edmond C. Gruss, *Apostles of Denial* (Nutley, NJ: Presbyterian and Reformed Publishing Co., 1970) on the Jehovah's Witnesses; Joseph Hopkins, *The Armstrong Empire* (Grand Rapids, MI: Eerdmans, 1974) which treats the Worldwide Church of God; Gordon R. Lewis, *Transcendental Meditation* (Glendale, CA: Regal, 1977); Floyd McElveen, *Will the "Saints" Go Marching In?* (Glendale, CA: Regal, 1977), on the Latter-day Saints (Mormons); Rachel Martin, *Escape* (Denver, CO: Accent Books, 1979), the Jim Roberts cult; and Thomas Whitfield, *From Night to Sunlight* (Nashville, TN: Broadman Press, 1980), the black Hebrews.

The New Age Movement, the Psychic and the Occult

Few topics have excited so much interest, and on occasion disagreement, as has the occult. A recent volume on the New Age Movement, *Hidden Dangers of the Rainbow* (1983) by Constance, Cumbey, though a best seller in Christian bookstores, is inadequate in its treatment, hence we can not recommend it. A balanced perspective on the psychic and occult which critically examines the issues and groups involved, yet does not lead Christians astray into an undo emphasis upon demons and demonology, is to be found in the best discussions on this phenomena. Two writers stand out for their balanced, Christian approach to the occult, John Warwick Montgomery and J. Stafford Wright. Montgomery's *Principalities and Powers* (Minneapolis, MI: Bethany Fellowship, 1973) and *Demon Possession* (Minneapolis, MN: Bethany Fellowship, 1976), and Wright's *Christianity and the Occult* (Chicago: Moody Press, 1972) and *Mind, Man and the Spirits* (Grand Rapids, MI: Zondervan, 1971), should satisfy even the most curious mind about the reality, the dangers, and a Christian assessment of what is popularly termed the psychic realm. While ably guiding the average church member through the intricate maze of occult phenomena, these books will strip the aura of fear which often surrounds them by a plain and simple divulging of basic information. In this same vein, Edmond C. Gruss, *The Ouija Board, Doorway to the Occult* (Chicago: Moody Press, 1975) is also an excellent introduction to the subject.

Danny Korem and Paul Meier's, *The Fakers* (Grand Rapids, MI: Baker Book House, 1980), as the name implies, goes one step further. They strip the aura of mystery and miracle from the occult realm by disclosing the stage magic which some professional psychics have used in faking psychic events. This is a good book for the gullible among us.

Within the realm of questions about the occult, some beliefs and practices have become popular topics beyond strictly occult circles. For example, life after death questions have led almost a fifth of the American public to adopt a belief in reincarnation. Of the very few books written from a Christian faith perspective on the subject, Mark Albrecht's *Reincarnation: A Christian Appraisal* (Downers Grove, IL: InterVarsity Press, 1982) is by far the best. It provides an excellent survey of the history of this belief, the phenomena associated with it, and a Christian response. Attention should also be given to an extremely well-written volume on the health issues surrounding the New Age Movement, *The Holistic Healers* by Paul C. Reisser, Teri K. Reisser, and John Weldon (Downers Grove, IL: InterVarsity Press, 1983).

Astrology surrounds the Christian everywhere, from the daily newspaper to the art work at department stores. The 1970s saw a major revival of astrology and a significant debate on its validity within the scientific community. Apart from understanding this debate, it is difficult to comprehend the modern "science of astrology" and its appeal. In defense of astrology, see *The Case for Astrology* by John Anthony West and Jan Gerhard Toonder (New York: Coward-McCann, 1970). For the argument against, see Michel Gauquelin's *The Dream and Illusion of Astrology* (Buffalo, NY: Prometheus Books,

1979). It should be noted that Guequelin's earlier writings on the correlation of professional careers and the position of planets at birth supplied a main building block in the defense of modern astrology. For a Christian interpretation, see James Bjornstad and Shildes Johnson, *Stars, Signs and Salvation in the Age of Aquarius* (Minneapolis, MN: Bethany Fellowship, 1971).

Some Scholarly Texts

Since the early 1970s, social scientists have brought their scholarly insights into an examination of cult phenomena. By the late 1970s, books summarizing their research began to appear and now supply a basic framework for understanding the nature of life in the cults and the role of cults in society. Two books stand out as scholarly appraisals of cults: David G. Bromley and Anson D. Shupe's, *Strange Gods* (Boston: Beacon Press, 1982) summarizes the sociological data and deals directly with many of the accusations made about cults by their more hostile critics. Robert S. Ellwood's *Alternative Altars* (Chicago: University of Chicago Press, 1979) gives a historical perspective of dissenting religion in America and shows the long presence in the country of what we sometimes call "new religions." Roy Wallis's *The Road to Total Freedom* (New York: Columbia University Press, 1977) is the best volume written by a critical observer of the Church of Scientology.

Three collections of essays on numerous cult related topics, many of which are not covered elsewhere, can be found in Irving I. Zaretsky and Mark P. Leone, *Religious Movements in Contemporary America* (Princeton, NJ: Princeton University Press, 1974); Jacob Needleman and George Baker, *Understanding the New Religions* (New York: Seabury Press, 1978); and Thomas Robbins and Dick Anthony, *In Gods We Trust* (Brunswick, NJ: Transaction Books, 1981). For those who seek a more historical approach to the cult problem, see Edwin Scott Gaustad, *Dissent in American Religion* (Chicago: University of Chicago Press, 1973) and Gustavus Myers, *History of Bigotry in the United States* (New York: Capricorn Books, 1960).

Further Resources: Publications and Workshops

Christians seeking additional information on specific groups are encouraged to contact the ministries specializing in Eastern religions, other non-Christian faiths, and groups whose teachings and practices deviate measurably from the orthodox Christian tradition. Without endorsing every resource printed or distributed by the following organizations, we have generally found their material most helpful when judged by the accuracy of information about the group under discussion, and their commitment to an evangelical faith perspective.

Spiritual Counterfeits Project
Box 4308
Berkeley, CA 94704

Evangelical Ministries to the New Religions
Dr. Gordon R. Lewis
Denver Conservative Baptist
  Seminary
Box 10,000
Denver, CO 80210

Personal Freedom Outreach
Box 26062
St. Louis, MO 63136

Christian Research Institute
Dr. Walter Martin
Box 500
San Juan Capistrano, CA 92693

The Institute for the Study of American Religion is an educational facility which has the most extensive collection of material on nonconventional religions in the United States. It specializes in informing the public and the church in general about different groups. Through its staff and board, it offers lectures, seminars and workshops on "The Cult Experience" to churches, schools, and other interested organizations. It is a valuable resource for checking on the accuracy of information about a specific group or gaining information about an otherwise unknown group. J. Gordon Melton, the Institute's director, conducts a personal ministry, separate from the Institute, to members of alternative religions and is available to speak to church groups. He may be contacted through the Institute at Box 5050, Evanston, IL 60204.

Ronald Enroth, in addition to teaching responsibilities, conducts seminars and workshops on the topic of contemporary cults for churches of all denominations and other Christian organizations. He may be contacted at: Westmont College, 955 La Paz Road, Santa Barbara, CA 93108.

APPENDIX

THE FLOWERING OF THE "NEW RELIGIOUS CONSCIOUSNESS"

FACTORS IN ITS SUDDEN GROWTH

J. GORDON MELTON

When the history of the 1970s and 1980s is written, future historians will undoubtedly see it as the time of the great religious transition—the time in which we as a people realized that the American experiment in freedom was producing an unimagined religious pluralism. These decades forced a vision of a time in which the dominance of Christianity in this country (which will remain for the foreseeable future) could be destroyed and replaced by a chaos of religious forms and spiritual infighting.

The fact of the matter is that during the last two decades we have witnessed the proliferation of alternatives to mainline Christianity in the appearance of several hundred religions that have immigrated to these shores from Asia and the Middle East. They have been joined by a number of new Christian variations that have become controversial because of their behavior (speaking in tongues, faith healing, etc.) or doctrinal heresy (denial of the divinity of Jesus). This proliferation of religions led to the creation in the early 1970s of two more groups, a militant anticult movement and a smaller but no less significant group of scholars who were fascinated by and in cases members and clients of the new religions. The new militant anticult movement, however, should not be confused with the century-old ministry of Christians witnessing to cult groups.

Both the anticultists and the new religions scholars agreed on two points. They overestimated, for exactly opposite reasons, the one to damn, the other to praise, the size and significance of these unfamiliar (to them) religions, and for the same opposing reasons overemphasized the discontinuity of the cults or new religions with previously-existing religious phenomena.

Neither the anticult nor the new religions perspectives with their emphasis upon the discontinuity of the phenomena offers an adequate approach from which to understand the pro-liferation of religious options during the recent past. A broader perspective based upon more careful attention to the demographic data and an appreciation of the history of the so-called "new religious consciousness," which has played such a significant role in American thought since the arrival of Sweden-borgianism in the eighteenth century and the absorption of Hinduism by New England intellectuals (Emerson, Thoreau, Alcott) in the nineteenth century, is needed. That broader perspective will provide the clues from which we can then locate the factors that contributed to the blossoming of the alternative religious forms during the last two decades.

American Religion in the 1970s

American religion experienced a major shift in power and position during the decade of the 1970s. While the nation's population grew, major liberal Protestant denominations ex-perienced a downtrend unprecedented in their life.[1]

	1971	1980
Christian Church (Disciples)	951,317	817,650

United Presbyterian Church	2,906,147	2,468,215
United Church of Christ	1,858,592	1,740,202
United Methodist Church	10,036,109	9,534,803

But where did these members go? They certainly did not flock to the new religions and alternative faiths. The overwhelming majority went to conservative evangelical Christian churches whose growth in recent decades represents another significant shift in American religious life. A million and a half Americans, for example, became charismatics, a fact reflected in the growth of some representative Pentecostal denominations:

	1971	*1980*
Assemblies of God	300,000	1,612,655
Church of God (Cleveland)	301,335	389,714
Pentecostal Holiness Church	72,720	100,000

In light of the mass movements with mainline church memberships, the alternative religions represent a relatively minor phenomena. Using the broadest definition, including such groups as the militant Ku Klux Klan-based Identity Movement churches, Black nationalist groups, and atheist-humanist associations (but excluding Asian and Middle Eastern immigrant groups that have made no attempt to adopt English or recruit from the English-speaking community), the alternative faiths are limited to less than five hundred different groups.[2] Many of these groups have less than one hundred members, most have less than a thousand. Only a few, such as the Unification Church, the International Society for Krishna Consciousness, the Divine Light Mission, and the Church Universal and Triumphant can count their members in the thousands. Very few—the Black Muslims, the Neo-Pagans, the Association for Research and Enlightenment (the Edgar Cayce group), and a few older movements such as Christian Science can count members in the tens of thousands.

Thus in terms of total membership the alternative religions

must still count members in the hundreds of thousands, not millions. A far larger number of people, of course, dabbled in alternative religious practices without any change of religious membership and/or faith commitment. Approximately one million people took the basic Transcendental Meditation course, though only a miniscule number attached themselves to the World Plan Executive Council. Some of that million were among the many thousands who took initiation from Guru Maharaj Ji and then failed to join the Divine Light Mission.[3]

While in terms of the major currents of American religion, alternative religions remain a relatively small eddy, they are nevertheless important. If not yet growing appreciably in numbers, the alternative religions have moved out of the narrow cultural and ethnic niches to which they have been largely confined and have now claimed a position in middle America. Their attraction of members still in their childbearing years means that they can expect continued growth from children who will grow up within the group itself. Before the end of the century the surviving groups will no longer have to rely entirely upon new converts for growth.

The last two decades have also seen the groups take major steps toward acceptance and even respectability in American culture. While the "cult wars" are by no means over, the new groups have found strong cultural allies among religious scholars, human potential psychologists, and the general public that has grown used to their presence over the past decade. During the 1970s the anticult movement massed its efforts in attempts to pass legislation, mobilize the public against the new religions, and deprogram group members. Instead it has come up with a legislative zero, a public little concerned with the cult threat, and a steady erosion of support for coercive deconversion.

What caused this movement of alternative religions into mid-America (the real drama of the past two decades)? It is to that question we now turn.

The Causes of Growth

Observers of the contemporary flowering of alternatives

have offered a wide variety of explanations about their growth. It will not be the task of this paper to review all of them, merely to point out the several prominent types of explanations and suggest a different direction for seeking an understanding of the phenomena.

One group of scholars has looked to broad cultural changes. For example, Wuthnow has suggested that an understanding of the new religions can occur only as "we examine the current transition in world order."[4] More recently, Anthony, Robbins, and Schwartz have suggested, "The emergence of new religions can be interpreted as the effect of a widespread perception in certain western societies of the inadequacy of scientific-technical rationalism alone to orient contemporary social life."[5] This hypothesis is a further expansion of an earlier suggestion that the new religions were the effect of the dissatisfaction of youth with the ideological and religious inconsistencies of modern society."[6]

This type of explanation, in either the more sophisticated and suggestive format offered by Wuthnow or the simpler assertation of Anthony, Robbins, and Schwartz, is not so much an explanation as an attempt to discern transitions within the larger society that provide a context within which the blossoming occurred and with which the various groups interacted. Such explanations, while possibly providing some insight about new religions, really describe the conditions faced by all religions and all religious people. They do not inform about proximate and direct causations and provide no answer to the basic question, "Why do some people (a minority) affected by the broad cultural forces choose to seek a solution in an alternative faith and the great majority seek and find it in either a more mainline setting or a nonreligious context?"

A second group of explanations draw causative factors from within the groups themselves. Tipton,[7] for example, sees the new groups as assisting their members to make moral sense of their lives. They needed to be saved from the turmoil of the 1960s. Needleman[8] suggests that a disillusionment with Judaism and Christianity coupled with an intensified spiritual quest brought on a response to the "new religious consciousness" supplied by the new religions.

This second group of explanations has its level of truth. The alternative religions among other accomplishments do supply their members with a moral framework and a different, if not new, religious consciousness. That in fact is what they claim to do and what members claim that they have received as a result of joining. However, all religions claim to provide these same two factors to members and always have. Thus neither explanation, nor others of this type, yield the factors for which we search. Why did a small group of those affected by the 1960s turn to alternative religions and the great majority turn elsewhere? Needleman's argument is further weakened by observation of the significantly larger numbers turning to conservative Christianity during the 1970s as opposed to those joining the new religions.

A third type of explanation has come from various anticult writers. They have suggested that the alternative religions are a new phenomenon in that they have perfected certain techniques to recruit and hold members. These techniques have been derived from Communist "brainwashing" and "thought reform" procedures that include "constant repetition of doctrine, application of intense peer pressure, manipulation of diet so that critical faculties are adversely affected, deprivation of sleep, lack of privacy and time for reflection, complete break with past life, reduction of outside stimulation and influences, the skillful use of ritual to heighten mystical experience and the invention of a new vocabulary and the manipulation of language to narrow the range of experience and construct a new reality." And, it is added, "These methods can bring about a complete personality transformation."[9]

I shall focus upon only one of the serious flaws in the anticult explanation at this point, namely the fact that to accept this hypothesis one must ignore the reality of centuries of religious life. The techniques used by the "new" religions are the same ones that have been used by religions both East and West throughout their lives, as is ably documented in even a cursory comparison of modern practice and ancient instructional material. Thus we acknowledge the anticult perspective not because it has any insight to offer but because it has received some popular support from those opposed to alternative religions for other reasons.

Toward a New Approach

In order to understand the current blossoming of new religions a brief historical background is necessary. Its necessity is suggested by the very hypothesis that generated the popular misnomer "new religions." The idea of a *new religious conscious-ness*, a perspective that the prominent alternative religions share, is a popular scholarly assumption. In her book *Cult and Countercult*, Scott has capably summarized this new religious consciousness.[10] In reading this summary, students of American alternative religions quickly realize that what has been called the *new* religious consciousness is identical in every respect with the *old* occult-theosophical teachings, which further suggests that the blossoming of the so-called new religions is based directly upon the earlier flowering of occult mysticism and Eastern thought that began in the nineteenth century.

The Alternative Religious Tradition in America

The emergence of the alternative religious tradition in the West is fittingly symbolized by the 1893 World Parliament of Religions, in which for the first time representatives of all the major world religions (and not a few minor ones) gathered for a six-weeks meeting for dialogue around a multiplicity of issues and a sharing of belief systems. Out of this meeting several alternative religions were formed. Swami Vivekananda, possibly the single most electrifying speaker at the Parliament, organized the first American Hindu group, the Vedanta Society. Buddhist Anagarika Dharmapala talked philosopher-editor Paul Carus into organizing the first American Buddhist group that sought members from among the general population, the Maha Bodhi Samaj. A few days after the Parliament Dharma-pala admitted the first Westerner into the Maha Bodhi Samaj at a Theosophical Society meeting.[11]

The Theosophical Society, which brought Annie Besant, possibly the second most charismatic speaker at the Parliament, held its last united gathering during those weeks. Soon after the Parliament ended, the American section under William Q. Judge bolted from the European and Indian branches and took most of the members with it. Judge died within a year of the schism, and the American section further divided. The four theosophical bodies present by 1900 would continue to divide and become the source for most of the occult bodies that appeared in the twentieth century.

The 1890s saw the first stable Spiritualist organization, the National Spiritualist Association of Churches, and the numerous metaphysical-New Thought groups that spread across the United States in the late twentieth century, form their first national organization, the International Divine Science Association. Its biannual conventions held throughout the decade from 1892 to 1899 attracted many New Thought leaders other than those who used the name "Divine Science." They led to the New Thought Convention in Hartford, Connecticut, in 1899. That convention culminated in the formation of the International New Thought Alliance in 1914.

By the end of the decade alternative religion had a broad national base with national organizations representative of the major Eastern faiths, the occult, Spiritualism, and New Thought. Once established, these organizations began a steady growth. Spiritualism, for example, often thought of as having its heyday in the nineteenth century, experienced a growth in the first half of the twentieth century hardly imagined possible by the many nineteenth century lecturers and local associations.

This first flowering of alternative religion did not happen without preparation. It built upon the long history of the two Swedenborgian Churches, Mesmerism, Spiritualism and psychical research, and Quimby's metaphysical students. Also not to be forgotten, in a country that could boast of only 35 percent of its population as church members, was the continuing popularity of folk magic in rural America and the introduction and spread of African magical religion (voodoo) in Louisiana.

And lest we come away with the notion that this alternative religious community grew among people alienated from the mainstream of American culture, let us take a quick look at the center of the alternative religious community in the 1880s —Boston and its environs.[12] This community was built around the prestigious Lowell Institute, which opened its halls to the dissemenation of a variety of new ideas, and the faculties of Harvard and Boston Universities. Most prominent among its leaders were the two sons of a devout Swedenborgian, William and Henry James. The former founded the American Society for Psychical Research in 1884 and brought many of America's intellectual elite such as Charles Sanders Peirce and Josiah Royce into it. Brother Henry was one of a number of the Boston intellectuals with more than a passing interest in Buddhism, an interest sparked by a set of lectures given in 1877 at the Lowell Institute by Harvard zoologist Edward Morse upon his return from Japan.

Around the James brothers could be found a growing following for Eastern religion. The Unitarian Church forged an alignment with several Hindu groups and brought the first Hindu teachers to America. Remembering the Transcendentalists' role in the Unitarian action, we note that when the first of these gurus, Protap Chundar Mozoomdar[13] came to America in 1883, he went directly to Concord. Emerson's widow opened her living room for his initial lecture. Also during the decade two Harvard professors, William S. Bigelow and Ernest Fenollosa, traveled to Japan where they were formally received into the Tendai Buddhist sect. Fenollosa had a major role in the Oriental movement in American art due both to his purchases of Oriental art and the art books he wrote.

Boston was, of course, home to Christian Science (founded in 1875) and the major students of Phineas P. Quimby—Annette and Horatio Dresser and Henry Felt Evans. Rev. Charles Cullis, the unknown fountainhead of the orthodox Christian healing movement, served a Boston parish. His work was picked up by two students of William James, Elwood Worshester and Samuel McComb, who would combine Cullis's interest in healing and James' interest in psychic phenomena to begin the Emmanuel Movement, the first successful healing movement to spread through the mainline churches, which survives today as the International Order of St. Luke the Physician.[14]

The Boston community also produced America's first astrological superstar, Evangeline Adams (from the prominent political family).[15] She became interested in astrology only after a prior adoption of an Eastern (Hindu) perspective given to her by Dr. J. Heber Smith. Smith, a nationally known diagnostician on Boston University's medical faculty, used astrology in his medical work. The growing astrological community included astronomer Joseph G. Dalton, who compiled one of the first American ephemerides, and Helen Taylor Craig, author of *The Stars and Your Destiny*, an early astrological best seller.

The development of an alternative religious community that could be said to have given its allegiance to what would later be termed the "new religious consciousness" did not end with the flowering in Boston or the institutionalization of the community in the 1890s. It grew steadily throughout the twentieth century. The Boston community illustrates how strongly Eastern religion, the occult, and New Thought metaphysics interacted with each other. Occult groups, by far the strongest segment of the community on a national level, became the avenue for introducing Eastern religion and thought to America. A basic notion of the alternative community was that occult wisdom could be found in Eastern esotericism. Prominent American advocates of Eastern thought arose at the turn of the century. New Thought leader William Walker Atkinson authored several New Thought classics but is best remembered for the volumes he penned under the pseudonym Yogi Ramacharaka. L. W. de Laurence, founder of the occult publishing company that bears his name, began life as a Hindu guru.

As Eastern teachers came to America, they sought out occult publishers such as the New York Magazine of Mysteries, and Yogi Publication Society, Samuel Weiser, and the Theosophical

Publishing House to spread their message. The Theosophical Society provided the major force for spreading Eastern thought. From its presses rolled the first books advocating (as opposed to merely examining) Eastern thought. Blavatsky standardized the term "reincarnation," which, until she became a popular writer and patron of occult writers, described a belief called by many names—transmigration, rebirth, metempsychosis, etc.

The steady growth of the alternative community was interrupted in the early part of the century by a series of oriental exclusion acts that cut immigration and denied potential citizenship to Asians already in America. The acts had two effects. First, they cut off the trickle of Eastern teachers coming to the United States and effectively limited the spread of Hinduism and Buddhism. Buddhist teachers allowed in were confined largely to serving the Japanese-American community. The few swamis established small Hindu movements: Baba Premanand Bharati (the Krishna Samaj); Yogi Hare Rama (the Benares League); Sri Deva Ram Sukul (Hindu Yoga Society); Swami Bhagwan Bissessar (Yogessar); Srimath Swami Omkar (Sri Mariya Ashrama); Kedar Nath Das Gupta (Dharma Mandala); Pierre Bernard (American Order of Tantriks); and Pundit Acharya (Yoga Research Institute).

The small amount of Buddhist work (primarily Zen) begun among Caucasians was completely disrupted by the internment of all their teachers during World War II.

Second, the exclusion of Asian teachers shifted the mode of transmission of Asian teaching. After World War I such teachings were filtered (and more or less distorted) through the writings of American occult teachers—Manly Palmer Hall, Alice Bailey, Edwin Dingle, and Gottfried de Purucker being a few prominent examples. The first half of the twentieth century is replete with Americans claiming secret Eastern wisdom, gathering disciples, and offering various mixtures of occult thought.

The Blossoming of the New Religious Consciousness

The development and lengthy history of the new religious consciousness prepared America for its blossoming during the

last two decades. The initial event that triggered the new efflu-
ence came as the culmination of a series of changes in Asia.
First, after World War II America imposed religious freedom on
Japan as a condition of peace. The new freedom resulted in the
rapid spread of many suppressed religious groups and the
founding of many more. Several hundred emerged within a
decade.

Second, in 1948 India attained its independence. As full
members of the British commonwealth, Indians had a freedom to
move and began to travel to England and Western Europe.
Among the travelers were swamis, gurus, and even a few avatars.

Third, following the Chinese Revolution, Hong Kong
swelled with refugees, many of whom were religious leaders
fleeing atheistic rule. It is this mass movement that leads directly
to the major event behind the current growth of Eastern religion.

In 1965 President Lyndon B. Johnson quietly rescinded the
Oriental Exclusion Act for the purpose of allowing the Hong
Kong immigrants to enter the United States. However, the consequences were staggering. In placing Asian immigration quotas on
a par with those of Western Europe, Johnson unleashed a massive
human movement. This legal change in the limits of Asian immigration is the single most important factor in the rise of new
religions, most of which are imports or schisms of importance.

The growth of new religions can be traced in the movement
of Eastern teachers to take up residency in the United States:

1965   Swami Bhaktivedanta
       Sant Keshavadas
       Thera Bope Vinita
1968   Yogi Bhajan
1969   Tarthang Tulku Rinpoche
1970   Swami Rama
1971   Swami Satchidananda
       Gurudev Chitrabhanu
       Maharaj Ji
1972   Sun Myung Moon (first visit in 1965)
       Vesant Paranjpe

Asian Religion's New Stance

When after half a century the obstacles to Asian immigration were lifted, Asian religions had changed, at least at one very important point. They were motivated by *a new missionary spirit.* Very much like the change that came over Christianity in the move from the eighteenth to the nineteenth century, an uncharacteristic missionary zeal developed among Hindus and Buddhists who set out to return the compliment paid them by Christian missionaries in previous decades.

Prior to the restrictions on Indian immigration only three swamis had been enthused enough to begin a Western Hindu thrust and only Vivekananda's work survived. Vivekananda's efforts were complemented in the 1920s by the work of Swami Yogananda and the few other gurus who slipped through the meager quotas allowed from India. Only Vivekananda and Yogananda found even miniscule support in India for their pioneering efforts. This lack of interest among Indians to convert Westerners is no better illustrated than in the case of Sikhism. Thousands of Sikhs crossed the Canadian-United States border illegally prior to 1965 and settled on the West Coast as agricultural workers. Being predominantly male and unable to bring potential wives from the Punjab, they intermarried with the local population, primarily Mexican-Americans. However, until Yogi Bhajan's appearance in 1968, fresh from the Punjab with a mission to evangelize the West, no American orthodox Sikh teacher had tried to proselytize among the non-Punjabi population.

Buddhism actually began a missionary attempt in the 1890s, but that move was *not* initiated by Asians. It resulted from the zeal of a Western convert, Col. Henry S. Olcott, the president of the Theosophical Society. Olcott's major ally was Anagarika Dharmapala, whom he encouraged to come to the World Parliament of Religions and to start the Maha Bodhi Samaj in America. But Olcott generated little response from other Buddhists, particularly the Japanese. It took Soyen Shaku, who also addressed the Parliament, a decade to convince his superiors that Westerners were ready and, more importantly, fit to receive the treasures of Buddhism. He was able to start and solidify a small Zen movement in California before the ax fell cutting off further immigration.

In recent decades, even Japanese Buddhism has absorbed the missionary spirit. The Soto Zen sect set up an English-language guest department to receive foreign students and train potential leadership. The Reformed Zen Church, headed by Jiyu Kennett-roshi is a direct result. After years of work in Japan, Kennett-roshi established a Soto mission as an outpost of the department in California. The sect also began to send roshis to America who were proficient in English. The first came in 1959 to take leadership of the old Soto temple in San Francisco. Without any prior response from the English-speaking community to build upon, Suzuki-roshi built within two years the San Francisco Zen Center, now one of the largest Zen communities in America.

The Hindu response to the new open-door policy has included an increase in the number of gurus receiving guidance to make the West the site of their labors. We can multiply the examples, but the conclusion would be the same—the United States and the West are experiencing a large-scale movement of both people and religion from East to West, a movement with the potential to remake the Western religious scene as significantly as the nineteenth-century Christian mission remade Africa and the Orient.

Western Response

The new missionary zeal in the East encountered a public situation greatly different from that of Vivekananda and Soyen Shaku in 1893. The American public had by 1965 been prepared for the spread of Eastern ideas both in the multiplication of academic courses in Eastern religion and the proliferation of books and other forms of information on Eastern teachings. No better measure of the growth of openness to Eastern ideas can be found than in the spread of the belief in reincarnation. In the 1880s when the Theosophical Society began to champion the idea in the West few supporters could be found. By the turn of the century it found strong non-Theosophical advocates, and in the 1920s it split non-Theosophical occult groups such as the Spiritualists and New Thought. By 1980, 23 percent of the American public professed belief. In the South, that area of the country least affected by the new religious consciousness, 32 percent of the black population is reincarnationist (5 percent higher than in California).

The spread of Zen, the first form of Buddhism to receive a popular response in America, can be traced directly to the appearance of English-language materials. Early in this century D. T. Suzuki translated a variety of Buddhist texts into English. These translations and others such as those in Dwight Goddard's *A Buddhist Bible* (1932), however, were not of the quality or type to attract a popular audience. Still they did provide material for a small group of highly-motivated people, among them Alan Watts. In 1956 Watts published *The Spirit of Zen*, a popular treatment of Suzuki's Zen, that found a ready public audience for a popular movement—Beat Zen.

The more successful gurus upon initiation of work in the United States would either come with a preexisting supply of books or quickly begin to print popular editions, the first step in a movement to the audio-visuals now widely employed by those groups wealthy enough to produce them.

Science into Religion

One final factor in the blossoming of the alternative religions and the new religious consciousness must be noted. Between the passing and rescinding of the Oriental Exclusion Act, some significant changes occurred in the scientific community. Three stand out for their crucial role in spreading the new religious consciousness.

First, in the 1930s parapsychology was born and, for many, superseded psychical research. Founder J. B. Rhine wanted to add a new methodology to the study of the paranormal, and the resulting efforts had some unexpected consequences, not the least of which has been the granting of previously-denied legitimacy to occult religions. The symbol of that new level of acceptance was the recognition of the Para-psychological Association as a full member of the American Association for the Advancement of Science.

Second, another scientific revolution began in 1938 when a Swiss chemist synthesized what came to be known as LSD. His later discovery of its mind-altering effects and the spread of the chemical through the scientific community after World War II set up a religious revival when several of the scientists turned from research to evangelism. The popular discovery of consciousness-altering chemicals and their widespread availa-bility, coupled with the identification of psychedelic experi-ences with religious experiences, seems to have strengthened the search for religion as an after effect of their imbibement.

The mainline churches as a whole opposed the use of psy-chedelic substances on moral grounds, while the alternative religions have tended to accept them (The Farm), be tolerant of them (most groups), or provide members with what they believe to be a better ecstasy (Hare Krishna, Jesus People).

Third, a revolution in psychiatry and psychology has pro-vided a new openness to alternative religions. The twentieth-century critique of Freud and Watson produced a number of alternative psychological systems, many of which have found a level of acceptance among professionals. Some of these systems took insights directly from the occult and in turn became legitimizing agents and tools of familiarization for alternative religions. The most prominent example, of course, is C. C. Jung, who became an accomplished student of the occult and whose thought, especially his concept of archtypes, gave a basic under-pinning to modern Neo-Paganism and magic.

Lesser known is Robert Assagioli, an Italian psychiatrist, who absorbed Theosophy and especially its revisionist presen-tation produced by Alice Bailey. His thought and the profes-sionals who practice his system, psychosynthesis, have become thoroughly intertwined with Bailey's Arcane School and its off-shoots.

On a broader scale humanistic psychology took a positive turn toward religion and religious experience. In connection with parapsychology it began to explore "peak experiences" and altered states of consciousness. Joined by Asian-trained psychologists, it gave birth to the human potential movement whose role as a bridge between more traditional psychology and alternative religions has been frequently noted.

Conclusion and a Proposal for Ministry and Missions

The blossoming of the "new religious consciousness" during the last two decades has not been produced by any recent or prominent shift in American, Western or world culture or consciousness. Rather, it resulted from the persistent and gradual spread of Eastern-mystical and occult religion since its rebirth in the late eighteenth century. Its growth has been punctuated by periodic bursts of new life such as was noted in the 1890s and through which American society has just passed. While the alternative religious community has not yet reached the point that it can seriously challenge the cultural hegemony of mainline churches or evangelical Christianity, it has fostered options that, if allowed to continue free of significant legal obstacles, can provide options which will increasingly gain the allegiance of middle America.

Prior to 1970, the metaphysical religious consciousness grew and spread largely unnoticed. Periodically religious observers reported the existence of leftover religions, those not included in the larger and more prominent Christian church families, but little understanding of the development and spread of a genuinely alternative religious vision permeating American life was evident. Thus, the noticeable growth of the alternative tradition in the 1970s caught many by surprise. Scholars called the alternative religions, "new religions." Anticultists, unaware of their role in American life since the founding of the republic, continued to treat them as a recent foreign intrusion into American culture.

The prevailing ignorance regarding the alternative religious tradition in America and the dominant image of the "new religious consciousness" has had a marked effect upon the structure of the Christian response to these religions. Not until the early twentieth century did Christian thinkers begin to alert the church that a number of alternative religions could be found throughout the land. When Van Baalen and his colleagues began to write, they picked up a new sociological category, "cult," a term used to describe marginal religions—those completely outside the Christian "Church-sect" patterns developed by Max Weber and Ernst Troeltsch. That model was passed to those church leaders who after World War II developed "counter-cult ministries," the dominant response to the increasing presence of non-Christian religion in the West. Over one hundred such ministries currently function in the United States alone.

Unfortunately, the development of ministries to what are perceived as marginal religious groups has tended to marginalize the ministries as well, and has delayed the recognition and acceptance by both mainline and evangelical denominations of the need for a mission strategy toward Eastern-metaphysical and occult religion in the West. The current counter-cult approach to these religions has become obsolete, and it should be replaced with both a new language and a new conceptualization of the developing situation.

The current marginalization of ministry to non-Christian religions in the West will not begin until such derogatory labels as "cult" are discarded. The alternative faith traditions are not aberrant forms of counterfeit faiths. They are, as a whole, Western representatives of the great Eastern and Middle Eastern religions, which, like Judaism, have been a small but important element in the West for the last two centuries. Adherents of these groups include people who have made a significant contribution to American life and culture: Ralph Waldo Emerson, Henry David Thoreau, Johnny Appleseed, William James, Abner Doubleday, Thomas Edison, Helen Keller, and Horace Greeley, to mention but a few. Not understanding themselves as marginal people, they participated fully in the American experiment in religious freedom. Their contemporary counterparts serve in high positions in business, politics, and the entertainment world.

Small, poorly-funded, marginalized, counter cult ministries

have had and can hope to have but minimal overall impact upon the continued growth and spread of the alternative faiths. Presently, in one state, one third of the residents are professing Buddhists. Islam has now replaced Judaism as the second largest non-Christan faith in America. Thirty percent of the American public accepts reincarnation. Over one fourth of all the religious denominations in the United States, though individually much smaller than competing Christian denominations, fit into the alternative religious families. In the face of this significant cultural phenomena, the small ministries must be content with occasional individual converts and divert a high percentage of their time away from ministry to fundraising and survival. Churches assign such ministries a low priority when judged by the enormity of other perceived world mission needs.

In the face of this marginalization, leaders of the counter-cult ministries, and sympathetic evangelical and mainline church leaders, must pool their collective resources and develop a new strategy which will engage the whole church in mission and ministry to non-Christian religions in the West. It will be painful to abandon present counter cult approaches. Yet only with a more comprehensive model, one which can mobilize the entire Christian community, can such ministries hope to achieve either a measurable impact on those currently affiliated with alternative religions, or have a voice in determining the coming necessary changes in public policy. Such a model need not be startingly new. The basics have already been provided in the documents from Lausanne, and an effort to bring the insights from Lausanne to bear on the counter cult ministries has already begun by the Evangelical Ministries to New Religions, an organization developed by Gordon Lewis at Denver Conservative Baptist Seminary.

It is beyond the scope of this paper to spell out the final elements of a new ministry and mission to non-Christians in the West. Such is not the task of any single person; it can only be accomplished by combining the insights of all those who have gained some expertise through the present counter cult ministries and others who are concerned with the problem. However, any such solution must take account of several vital areas, beginning with the claims of Christ and the Christian gospel in its universal dimension over each person's life. Preaching the gospel effectively is the initial element in the new model. Recognition of the new religious situation should be analyzed, not as the work of the devil launched against the Christian West, but rather as the God-given opportunity to preach the good news to an until now neglected segment of the population. However, other questions of almost equal importance immediately arise. The model must speak insightfully to the issues of an emerging pluralistic religious culture of the West. It must create a strategy to assist in the direction of public policies concerning religion in those areas where religious pluralism impinges upon the political, economic, educational and legal spheres. Education of Christian youth in world religion environment must receive some priority and educators be directed to produce the necessary church school materials. Such materials must not only inform about the beliefs and practices of different religions, but teach human relations skills for Christian youth who must grow up and survive in a pluralistic culture.

The Christian church is a large community with vast material resources. Evangelicals with this body now number over forty million strong. Yet the task before the church is enormous. Only men and women faithfully dedicating their spiritual, physical, and mental abilities to that task, and drawing upon the strength and guidance of the Holy Spirit as they labor, can be equal to it.

Appendix
Notes

1. Figures were derived from various editions of the *Yearbook of American Churches*, Douglas W. Johnson, Paul R. Ricard and Bernard Quinn, *Churches and Church Membership in the United States* (Washington, DC: Glenmary Research Center, 1971), and Bernard Quinn et al, *Churches and Church Membership in the United States* (Washington, DC: Glenmary Research Center, 1980).

2. This information is derived from the files of the Institute for the Study of American Religion, which is currently surveying the alternative religions for a new edition of *The Encyclopedia of American Religions*.

3. During the early 1970s I became aware of the large number of people who carried dual memberships in a selection of what Stark and Bainbridge call client cults. As the national field director for Spiritual Frontiers Fellowship I observed members who also had joined the Association for Research and Enlightenment, the Theosophical Society, the American Society for Psychical Research, and other psychic interest groups, all in addition to their home church in a mainline denomination.

4. Robert Wuthnow, "Religious Movements and the Transition in World Order," in Jacob Needleman and George Baker, eds., *Understanding the New Religions* (New York: Seabury, 1978), p. 65.

5. Dick Anthony, Thomas Robbins, and Paul Schwartz, "Contemporary Religious Movements and the Secularization Premise," in John Coleman and Gregory Baum, eds., *New Religious Movements* (New York: Seabury, 1983), p. 7.

6. Dick Anthony and Thomas Robbins, "The Effect of Detente on the Growth of New Religions: Reverend Moon and the Unification Church," in Jacob Needleman and George Baker, eds., *Understanding the New Religions* (New York: Seabury, 1978), p. 80.

7. Steven M. Tipton, *Getting Saved from the Sixties* (Berkeley: University of California Press, 1982).

8. Jacob Needleman, *The New Religions* (Garden City: Doubleday, 1970).

9. James Rudin and Marcia Rudin, *Prison or Paradise* (Philadelphia: Fortress Press, 1980), pp. 16-17.

10. Gini Graham Scott, *Cult and Countercult* (Westport, CT: Greenwood, 1980), pp. 11-14.

11. Cf. Rick Fields, *How the Swans Came to the Lake* (Boulder, CO: Shambhala, 1981).

12. For a discussion of the Boston community in the 1880s from a Buddhist perspective, see Fields, *op. cit.*, pp. 146ff.

13. Suresh Chunder Bose, *The Life of Protap Chunder Mozoomdar* (Calcutta: Nababidhan Trust, 1940).

14. Sanford Gifford, *The Emmanuel Movement, Medical Psychotherapy and the Battle over Lay-Treatment, 1906-1912*. 1974 revised manuscript in the Institute for the Study of American Religion collection.

15. Evangeline Adams, *The Bowl of Heaven* (New York: Blue Ribbon Books, 1926).